THE AMERICAN SCENE

The American Scene

Essays on Nineteenth-Century American Literature

Stuart Hutchinson

Senior Lecturer in English and
American Literature
University of Kent at Canterbury

St. Martin's Press   New York

First published in the United States of America in 1991

Printed in Hong Kong

ISBN 0–312–06134–X

Library of Congress Cataloging-in-Publication Data
Hutchinson, Stuart.
    The American scene: essays on nineteenth-century American
literature / Stuart Hutchinson.
        p.   cm.
    Includes bibliographical references (p.   ) and index.
    ISBN 0–312–06134–X
    1. American literature—19th century—History and criticism.
I. Title.
PS201.H8   1991   90–28500
810.9'003—dc20   CIP

Contents

Contents

Acknowledgements

All students of nineteenth-century American literature are indebted to a number of well-known American literary critics. The writings of Chase, Fiedler, Feidelson, Matthiessen, Poirier and Winters have especially influenced me.

This book has been written while I have been teaching English and American literature at the University of Kent at Canterbury. I would like to thank my colleagues and the University for providing the context for a book of this kind.

Quotations of Emily Dickinson's poetry are reprinted by permission of the publishers and the Trustees of Amherst College from *The Poems of Emily Dickinson*, edited by Thomas H. Johnson, Cambridge, Mass.: The Belknap Press of Harvard University Press, copyright 1951, © 1955, 1979, 1983 by the President and Fellows of Harvard College; and by permission of Little, Brown and Company from *The Complete Poems of Emily Dickinson* edited by Thomas H. Johnson. Copyright 1929 by Martha Dickinson Bianchi; copyright © renewed 1957 by Mary L. Hampson.

Introduction

The common aim of all the works discussed in this book is to articulate whatever relationship there is between the self and the New World. This act of articulation is a genesis, because what has been said about the self and the Old World does not serve in the New. The literary precedents are for materials American writers do not have. For the materials they do have there are no precedents at all.

To be on the ocean with Ishmael, on the river with Huck, or moving from word to word in a Dickinson poem, is hardly to know where we began, where we are going, where we will end. There is a fundamental indeterminacy which is also formal instability. The self within the text does not know what to be, and the text itself does not know what to be.

Cooper is an exception to this indeterminacy and elsewhere there are pretensions to identity and design. Whitman proclaims that the self, the world and his poems express a transcendent purpose. Along with Melville, he also invokes organic form in which everything finds its natural shape. Hawthorne concedes to Original Sin as a determining force. Poe and James propose the authority of art itself. None of the theses is unique to nineteenth-century American literature, but none elsewhere has as big a space to fill.

It is a New World space without the Old World middle ground on which imagination and reality, what the self wants and what it can get, can be reconciled. In this American scene, the self finds no accommodation; even its humor is unsettled and unsettling.

1
Cooper: *The Leather-Stocking Tales*

I

No other American writer in this book has Cooper's assurance about the authorial self, the New World and the reader. We see this assurance in the opening paragraph of *The Pioneers* (1823), the first of *The Leather-Stocking Tales*. It amounts to an affirmation of America's cultural continuity with Britain. In the New World, so the opening paragraph of *The Pioneers* implies, are 'beautiful and thriving villages'[1] and 'neat and comfortable farms', of which the Old World itself might be proud. America is independent, but its expectations are reassuringly traditional:

> The expedients of the pioneers who first broke ground in the settlement of this country are succeeded by the permanent improvements of the yeoman, who intends to leave his remains to molder under the sod which he tills, or, perhaps, of the son, who born in the land, piously wishes to linger around the grave of his father. Only forty years have passed since this territory was a wilderness.

These traditional structures and values are reciprocally enacted in the complete Anglicisation of Cooper's prose. As for the reader, this baffling figure for other nineteenth-century American writers is unproblematic for Cooper. *The Leather-Stocking Tales*, according to the 1850 Preface, are intended for 'an enlightened and cultivated reader's notice'.

Because Cooper is so secure, even his account of 'the poverty of [literary] materials'[2] in America has, in Leslie Fiedler's words, something 'merely conventional' about it, and is not the 'cry from the heart'[3] of similar pronouncements by Hawthorne, Melville and James. Likewise in *The Pioneers*, the description in Chapter 3 of the problems arising from building Judge Temple's house according to

1

'English architecture' is mainly intended to amuse. It is written with the affectionate indulgence of someone who is sure he and his readers are not worryingly implicated in such confusions. Its message about the likely inappropriateness of constructing the New World in Old World forms apparently casts no doubt on Cooper's confidence in his own imported literary manners and values.

As we might expect, this unquestioning authorial security is complicitous in the limited range of *The Leather-Stocking Tales*. Although Elizabeth Temple responds with 'mute wonder' (Chapter 3) to the pace and scale of change, which are referred to several times in *The Pioneers*, no one experiences the problems of dislocation that Hawthorne presents in *The Scarlet Letter* (especially in 'The Custom-House' Prelude) and James in *The American Scene*. The possible inconsequence of life in the middle of nowhere renders no one murderous, as it does Colonel Sherburn in Chapter 21 of *Huckleberry Finn*. The essential range of Cooper's response in *The Pioneers* to the shaping of the New World is indicated in Judge Temple's 'mingled feeling of pleasure and desolation' (Chapter 21), when he first viewed the virgin forest and shores of the lake which were to become Templeton. On the one hand, the judge looks forward, with Cooper, to endowing the New World with 'all the . . . resources of an old country' (Chapter 29). On the other hand, both the judge and Cooper will always remain sympathetic towards Natty Bumppo, because they share Natty's melancholy over the despoiling of what Natty terms 'a second paradise' (Chapter 26).

Even this phrase, 'second paradise', secures the New World in what is revealed as an unproblematic Old World structure of comprehension. Natty cannot abide civilisation's encroachment on the woods, but he is no Ishmael from *Moby-Dick* or Huck from *Huckleberry Finn*. His quitting of civilisation is not a compulsive, unrewarded search for his true destination. Natty is completely at one with the judge and Cooper in believing the New World to be always reassuringly part of God's creation. What one misses in this generally untroubled conviction is the challenge of experiencing the New World as something alien and unknown. I think, for example, of Whitman and, 'the large unconscious scenery of my land with its lakes and forests'.[4] Oppressed to the point of despair by this unconsciousness, Whitman too needed to come up with the presence of God. Yet his God, in whatever form it is manifest, is a radical God for the New World. It is never the conventional God complacently invoked by Natty, with authorial support, from *The Pioneers* to *The Deerslayer* (1841): 'None know how often the hand of God is seen in the wilderness, but them that roves it for a man's life' (Chapter 25).

Although Cooper was a Christian, he shared with Natty Bumppo, in Fiedler's words, 'an immunity to Calvinism and its vestigial influences rare among American writers'. Fiedler concludes: 'It is perhaps because the doctrine of original sin has lost for [Cooper] . . . all effective force that his novels fail finally to achieve a tragic dimension.' Even Cooper's ambivalence towards the exploitation of the wilderness is always too resolvable to reach to tragedy. The justly famous and vividly presented pigeon-shooting scene in Chapter 22 of *The Pioneers* comes down to the message that it is wrong to use natural resources wastefully. On a line stretching from Billy Kirby and Richard Jones, who represent the forces of civilisation unrestrained, to Natty and Chingachgook, by whom nature is engaged only for immediate personal sustenance, there is the achievable middle ground occupied by Judge Temple, with the aim of husbanding natural resources and enabling a developing society to thrive. We may lose our footing and fall from this ground, as the judge does in this episode, but it is always recoverable and has been recovered in the novel's opening paragraph, where Cooper himself stands. In the *Moby-Dick* chapter, 'Stubb Kills a Whale', by contrast, the life of humanity is genuinely tragic, because, in search for the light, we are led to such appalling acts of slaughter. No middle ground will ever resolve what, whether we are religious or not, we may continue to regard as the continuing original sin of our existence.

I am not saying that the only significant literature is tragic literature. It is rather that Cooper ceases to explore conflicts, presented as integral to his material, at the very points where his certainties might falter. In Chapter 2 of *The Pioneers* he begins his account of Judge Temple's past with an epigraph from Shakespeare's *Richard II*:

> All places that the eye of heaven visits
> Are to a wise man ports and happy havens. . . .
> Think not the king did banish thee,
> But thou the king.[5]

The words are John of Gaunt's to his banished son, Henry Boling-broke. During *Richard II* the latter will eventually return from banishment, usurp the throne from Richard and, as a result of this act, become the guilt-ridden and tragic king of two succeeding plays. The epigraph, therefore, might have borne with some significance on the career of the judge and on his part in a revolution which overthrew in America the power of an English king. We are told that the judge committed himself completely 'in the cause, as it was then called, of the rebellion' and, during the resulting war, never lost sight of his own interests: 'When the estates of the adherents of the crown fell under the hammer by the acts of confiscation, he appeared in New York and became the purchaser of extensive possessions at comparatively low prices' (Chapter 2). These possessions originally belonged to his royalist friend, Effing-ham, from whom the judge becomes divided.

America, therefore, was founded in an ominous conflict in which, if *Richard II* is to be brought to bear on the matter, it could be argued that both parties, as in the play, were in the right. The epigraphs Cooper takes from Shakespeare, however, never draw significantly on the creative and dramatic energy of particular plays. This is even the case with the recurrent allusions in *The Last of the Mohicans* (1826) to *The Merchant of Venice*, while during *The Prairie* (1827) the plays from which various epigraphs are taken cease to be identified. For Cooper the epigraphs function only as a treasury of epigrammatic sayings, giving clues, as sayings, to situations in his books. They are also another assertion that Britain and America inherit a common culture.

As a patriot, Cooper was in any case not disposed to cast any serious doubts on the judge's part in the War of Independence, or on the morality of the judge's expediency. Nor, in so far as the judge was a representation of his father, was he disposed to feel, as Hawthorne did with respect to his forbears, ancestral guilt. His phrasing ('in the cause, as it was then called, of the rebellion') indicates that, from his perspective in the 1820s as he writes the book, he would rather not recognise the American 'rebellion' as a rebellion. To continue to do so might risk associating it with the French Revolution, for which neither he nor the judge (see Chapters 8 and 20) has any sympathy.

The message of *The Pioneers* is that all conflicts over possession and dispossession (between Red Indians and Whites, Old World and New World) can be reconciled. So desirous is Cooper that

America be accepted into the fold of established nations inhabited by enlightened and cultivated readers, that he writes as if the War of Independence had never happened. He writes what the 1850 Preface terms 'romances'. For the most part in *The Leather-Stocking Tales*, as I shall argue later, 'romances' means excursions and adventures away from reality in a country which, in the words of *The Pioneers'* first paragraph, 'eminently possesses' a 'romantic and picturesque character'. It is this Cooper that Twain so devastatingly pillories in 'Fenimore Cooper's Literary Offenses' (1895).

II

Twain does not refer to *The Pioneers* and in this respect is unfair to Cooper. In its presentation of events in the life of Templeton during the changing seasons of a year, *The Pioneers* has more substance than the other Tales, while the range of character-types makes Templeton a representative New World beginning. Chapters 14 (in the 'Bold Dragon'), 17 (the turkey-shoot), 22–24 (pigeon-shooting and fishing) are especially outstanding. It is sometimes claimed that The Leather-Stocking Tales are only source-books for ideas about America. In these chapters, major themes of American experience are expressed creatively in the realisation of scene, incident and character.

Not that one should make too much of these claims, even when the tediousness of Cooper (for example, in Chapter 6 with Dr Elnathan Todd) is forgotten. As Lawrence says of *The Pioneers* in an enlivening essay on *The Leather-Stocking Tales*: 'It is all real enough. Except that one realises that Fenimore was writing from a safe distance, where he could idealise and have his wish-fulfilment.'[6] What Lawrence means is exemplified even by the fishing episode, when Leather-Stocking (Natty) and Mohegan (Chingachgook) come into view with that Donald Davie[7] justly recognises as symbolic light:

The light suddenly changed its direction, and a long and slightly built boat hove up out of the gloom, while the red glare fell on the weather-beaten features of the Leatherstocking, whose tall person was seen erect in the frail vessel, wielding, with the grace of an experienced boatman, a long fishing spear, which he held by its center, first dropping one end and then the other into the water, to aid in propelling the little canoe of bark, we will not say through, but over, the water. At the further end of the vessel a form was faintly seen, guiding its motions, and using a paddle with the ease of one who felt there was no necessity for exertion. The Leatherstocking struck his spear lightly against the short staff which upheld, on a rude grating framed of old hoops of iron, the knots of pine that composed the fuel, and the light, which glared high, for an instant fell on the swarthy features and dark glancing eye of Mohegan.

(Chapter 24)

This picture of the manner of Leatherstocking's and Mohegan's fishing obviously creates a contrast to the 'wasteful extravagance' of the judge's party in the previous chapter. The whole fishing episode re-enacts themes already dramatised in the pigeon-shooting scenes. Throughout *The Pioneers*, Cooper is debating the morality of civilisation's incursion on nature, together with the laws civilisation imposes on the individual's natural desire for freedom.

As does the pigeon-shooting scene, the fishing episode complicates these issues by revealing Leatherstocking and Mohegan, who wish to remain free of civilisation, to be nonetheless upholders of restraint. The judge's party, however, while they affirm civilisation's law and order, indulge in unrestraint. The episode is thus an example of how *The Pioneers* maintains interest in its fixed and undeveloping character-types by subjecting them to different forces, so as to illustrate apparent contradictions. Later, the judge's personal relief that Leatherstocking's prowess amid nature saved his daughter in the forest fire is also his public condemnation of this same prowess which urged Leatherstocking to kill a deer out of season. Furthermore, any society needing to husband its natural resources for the benefit of all will eventually need to restrain both a Natty who kills a deer out of season and, as Chapter 20 makes clear, a Billy Kirby who thoughtlessly chops down trees. From this point of view, Leatherstocking and Kirby, characters in opposite positions, become characters in the same position.

As far as their individual lives are concerned, however, and paying no attention to larger communal needs, Leatherstocking's and Mohegan's whole manner of existence is a version of that 'life in harmony with nature'[8] which was also varyingly expressed as an ideal by later nineteenth-century American writers. In its articulation of a harmonious relationship between the self and the

New World, the manner of this life amounts to a minimisation of humanity's intrusive powers. So, the 'frail vessel' of 'bark' glides 'we will not say through, but over the water', and attention is drawn to Leatherstocking's 'grace'. Without 'exertion', Mohegan, who is assumed to be a savage at a far remove from civilisation, guides the whole venture.

Every student of nineteenth-century American literature who begins to think about Leatherstocking and Mohegan will also be at least reminded of Ishmael and Queequeg, and Ahab and Fedallah, in *Moby-Dick*. As American writers tried to define the self in relationship to the New World, we can see how necessary it was that the definition should include relationship with non-European races. What the relationship would amount to was very much dependent on the nature of the work in question. In a book of radically explorative energy such as *Moby-Dick*, Ishmael's and Ahab's respective relationships, however intermittently presented, would themselves be radical. Ishmael's is with a proud pagan; Ahab's with a Parsee, who is as ready as Ahab himself to encounter creation's apparent diabolism.

Throughout *The Leather-Stocking Tales*, Cooper's treatment of the Red Indians is altogether less adventurous. In the last quotation from the fishing episode, it is noticeable how his prose concedes none of its civilised manners, even as it presents a life in harmony with nature. 'We will not say through, but over, the water', writes Cooper. The 'we' invites the civilised reader, whom Cooper is always sure he has in his possession, to be complicitous in indulging the book. It invites us to regard the scene not as a possible life that might challenge our own, but as a composed picture, a confessed and indulged ideality, or, to refer back to Lawrence, a 'wish-fulfilment'. Similarly, the adjective 'rude' is too easy and sentimental. It allows us to regard Leatherstocking and Mohegan as untainted by civilisation (an effect Cooper wants), but it also suggests they are unskilled (an effect Cooper does not want).

The vital life of Leatherstocking and Mohegan, equal to that of the nature itself, is at its most rebellious against Judge Temple's civilisation in the exciting deer-killing episode in Chapter 27:

Natty, bending low, passed his knife across the throat of the animal, whose blood followed the wound, dyeing the waters . . . he laughed in his peculiar manner: 'So much for Marmaduke Temple's law!' he said.

At this climax, Mohegan, who has 'long been drooping with his years', is momentarily re-invigorated and pronounces the benediction, 'Good'. Bearing in mind that Judge Temple was a version of Cooper's father, one feels very persuaded at this juncture by Henry Nash Smith's Freudian judgement: 'If the father rules, and rules justly, it is still true that in this remembered world of his childhood Cooper figures as the son. Thus he is able to impart real energy to the statement of the case for defiance and revolt.'[9]

The eventual trial, however, conclusively dissipates the defiance and revolt. No one seriously interested in questioning justice and the law would have chosen from *King Lear* (think what is available!) the particular lines used as epigraphs to Chapters 33 and 34. In the deer killing episode, moreover, it is noticeable how Mohegan can only experience a revification of energies which are fading. The prevailing sense of him is one of obsolescence, as he conceals 'the shame of a noble soul, mourning for glory once known' (Chapter 7).

As Fiedler has observed, this elegy for the noble savage serves to appease Cooper's white guilt over the dispossession of the Indian. In compliance with this dispossession, and as a further dilution of his independent force, Mohegan has allowed himself to be 'Christianized' (Chapter 12). It is doubtful if the author could bear Mohegan any other way. Cooper is no bloodless Louisa Grant in response to the Indian, but as Mohegan's dark, fiery eyes preside over Leatherstocking's fishing and deer killing, and tell elsewhere of 'passions unrestrained and thoughts free as air' (Chapter 12); as Mohegan's countenance in the 'Blue Dragon' assumes 'an expression very much like brutal ferocity' (Chapter 14), one senses Cooper becoming unnerved. A day-dream of the noble savage can become a nightmare of the savage embodying a state of subhumanity, such as we meet in the 'bad' Indians in *The Last of the Mohicans*. Paradoxically, therefore, Mohegan must die at the end of *The Pioneers*, both because he is the noble savage rendered obsolete by civilisation, and also because he hints at what Cooper sees as our unregenerate savage nature, which civilisation is intended to redeem and replace.

Mohegan has been a lifelong companion of Leatherstocking, but it is ultimately on Leatherstocking's white terms. Even though Cooper can allow us to believe in the tavern scene in Chapter 14 that white civilisation degraded Mohegan (in this case through alcohol), there is no recognition that Mohegan might speak for an equivalent civilisation which was *not* savage. Similarly, *The Pioneers* itself settles all its conflicts on white terms. After misleading us about Oliver Edwards' Indian blood, it fiddles the issue by revealing his grandfather had been made an honorary member of the Delawares. At this point the judge exclaims: 'This, then, is thy Indian blood?' In reply we read: '"I have no other," said Edwards, smiling' (Chapter 40).

'I'll try a pagan friend, thought I, since Christian kindness has proved but hollow courtesy.' In contrast to this avowal by Ishmael in the chapter, 'A Bosom Friend', Leatherstocking will keep Mohegan in touch with Christianity. As the Indian finally determines to die in the fire sweeping through the forest, Leatherstocking's command is: 'Up and away, Chingachgook! Will ye stay here to burn, like a Mingo at the stake? The Moravians have teached ye better, I hope' (Chapter 37). Here, 'Mingo' refers to the degenerate Indian savages we are to meet in later Tales. When Leatherstocking's plea fails, he carries Mohegan to safety. Like Marlow desperately going after Kurtz when he is crawling back into the jungle in *Heart of Darkness* (1902), Leatherstocking cannot bear what he sees as an act of regression. Although the Indian eventually dies looking westward and seeing 'no white skins' (Chapter 38), Leatherstocking has him buried with his head laid reconcilingly 'to the east'. The epitaph reads: 'His faults were those of an Indian and his virtues those of a man' (Chapter 40). Author and characters find this pronouncement entirely appropriate.

It is not surprising that they should, since the only protest Cooper has allowed Mohegan (Chapter 36) is that he has lived the white man's God better than has the white man himself. How we miss something like the passionate protest voiced by Caliban in *The Tempest*: 'This island's mine, by Sycorax my mother, / Which thou tak'st from me.'[10] *The Pioneers* follows *The Tempest* in arriving at a final reconciling marriage of the children of enemies, but it cannot risk the atavistic resistance to such a structure which Shakespeare, out of sheer creative instinct, lets loose even in a most diagrammatic play. Nor should Leatherstocking's final quitting of civilisation be thought to be the equal of Huck's compulsion at the end of *Huckleberry Finn* 'to light out for the Territory'. Leatherstocking after all is only leaving civilisation, so that he can settle in the woods for a better version of civilisation's upholding faith. Huck is lighting out because, as the very form of *Huckleberry Finn* asserts, there is nothing to be settled for.

III

Before I comment on the later *Leather-Stocking Tales*, I want briefly to discuss Cooper and Scott, and the nature of the Tales when compared especially to Scott's *Waverley* (1814). Cooper has always been associated with Scott,[11] whose *Waverley* is credited with being the first historical novel or historical romance.

That *Waverley* can be seen as novel and romance complicates the discussion. The two categories are never easy to distinguish, and Scott's 'An Essay on Romance' (1824) acknowledged that some prose narratives would indeed belong to both. In the essay he defined romance as 'a fictitious narrative in prose or verse; the interest of which turns upon marvellous and uncommon incidents'. The novel, by contrast, was 'a fictitious narrative, differing from the romance, because the events are accommodated to the ordinary train of human events, and the modern state of society'.[12] This was the distinction Hawthorne was to redeploy in the Preface to *The House of the Seven Gables* (1851).

In *Waverley*, the 'marvellous and uncommon' romance elements are very much to do with what the central character, Edward Waverley, experiences among the Highlands and Highlanders of mid-eighteenth-century Scotland. Visiting this strange territory, Waverley, the young impressionable Englishman of sensibility, is very much a surrogate for the reader. Like Lockwood arriving in remote Yorkshire in *Wuthering Heights* (1847), he is very susceptible to the 'marvellous and uncommon'. From Scott, Emily Brontë learned that what might be termed romance material could be all the more effective, if it were filtered to the reader through a central character who, in strange circumstances, was understood to be looking for romance wherever he could find it, and who would find more than he initially sought. Melville uses the same tactic intermittently in the opening chapters of *Moby-Dick*.

What Waverley encounters among the Highlanders is a Scottish culture remarkably distinct from his Englishness and passionately expressed in the Jacobite uprising of 1745. The ambivalent form of *Waverley* is Scott's own ambivalence towards this 'marvellous and uncommon' period in the past, and towards 'the modern state of society'. Even as the latter commands all Scott's moral and intellectual allegiance, the defeat of the former is experienced as a great loss.

Romance for Cooper has none of the complications it has for Scott, let alone for Hawthorne. On the whole it is no more than an occasion for the 'marvellous and uncommon' becoming the frankly incredible. We have adventures for the sake of adventures: dangers and more dangers, rescues and more rescues. As critics point out, no one can believe of *The Last of the Mohicans* that Heyward would ever have set out in wartime on that journey with Cora and Alice, nor have chosen as a guide an Indian, whom the father of the girls has had publicly 'whipped like a dog' (Chapter 11[13]) for drunkenness. Likewise, in *The Prairie*, it makes no sense to kidnap Inez for ransom and take her into remote territory from where her family cannot be contacted.[14]

Cooper suffers too in comparison to Scott, when it comes to the issues of *The Leather-Stocking Tales*. He has no more than a very diluted version of Scott's ambivalence because, unlike Scott with the Highlanders, he can give very little substance to any world that might be an alternative to the world he has settled for. As alternatives to this 'modern state of society', Cooper has only the world of the Indians, about which he can do little more than offer fantasy, and Natty's and Chingachgook's life, with which his imagination comes to a halt almost as soon as it begins. In writing of Natty and Chingachgook and the 'stark, stripped human relationship of two men, deeper than the deeps of sex', Lawrence clearly looses contact with Cooper and re-enters the putative relationship of Rupert Birkin and Gerald Crich in his own *Women in Love* (1921).

Unlike Scott, Cooper makes little of his historical material, though he is very precise with dates. When there are wars, they have only a circumstantial, background effect. A possible difference between a French New World and a British New World is settled simply by making the French and their Indians bad. As for America independent or America British, this becomes a non-issue when America independent is imagined to be rather the same as America British. *The Last of the Mohicans: A Narrative of 1757* begins indeed with criticism of Britain for having let its colonies down.

As the date in the subtitle indicates, *The Last of the Mohicans*, to which I shall now turn, is set forty years earlier than *The Pioneers*. Consequently, we meet a much younger Natty (Hawk-eye) and Chingachgook. In Chapter 3, when we first come into their presence, they are deliberating over what Marlow at the beginning of *Heart of Darkness* is to term 'the conquest of the earth'. As in

Conrad's novella, this process is seen fatalistically as an unending one. Chingachgook's tribe had once been all-conquering, fighting 'the Alligewi, till the ground was red with their blood'. Now, they in their turn have been dispossessed by the incoming whites. The result is that Chingachgook and his son, Uncas, are the last of Chingachgook's people. Uncas is the last of the Mohicans.

As in *The Pioneers*, Chingachgook faces the extinction of his people, which Cooper presents as impersonal history but which is entirely the author's personal romance, with a melancholy and a resignation that mutes all protest. With respect to the Indian, the 'savage', *The Last of the Mohicans* is indeed a full orchestration of ideas emerging in *The Pioneers*. The Indian is now divided in two: good and bad. As we discover in the opening paragraphs of Chapter 6, Uncas is the noble savage. Magua, his counterpart, is throughout the treacherous savage, some of whose followers are sub-human.

Cora, who is given a twist of black blood to make her passions understandable and to distinguish her from Alice, her half-sister with 'fair golden hair, and bright blue eyes' (Chapter 1), is instinctively attracted to both Uncas and Magua. What might be a noble relationship with the former, however, would, in her eyes, be 'horror' (Chapter 1) and 'degradation' (Chapter 11) with the latter. Strangely, it would not be degradation for an Indian girl to be Magua's bride, as is made plain by Cora when, in Chapter 11, she responds to his 'revolting' proposal to herself.

Cooper supports Cora in the chapter by over-insisting on Magua's irredeemably evil nature. He is described as 'fiercely malignant', as having a 'malignant laugh' and 'tones of deepest malignancy', and as being inclined to 'malignant enjoyment'. Moreover, he is a self-betrayer and a self-degrader. Whereas in *The Pioneers* it is possible to believe that Mohegan is the victim of white man's alcohol, when Magua tells how 'his Canada fathers came into the woods, and taught him to drink fire-water, and he became a rascal', there is very little to mitigate what is seen as his racial weakness and culpability, and Cooper himself writes of his 'supposed injuries'. As for Magua's followers, they are at this stage as disgusting as the Yahoos in *Gulliver's Travels* (1726), though there is none of Swift's irony in presenting this condition. While Magua outlines his schemes to Cora, they make a 'revolting meal' from an uncooked fawn. Later in the chapter, they are presented as a 'cluster of lolling savages, who, gorged with their disgusting meal, lay, stretched on the earth, in brutal indulgence'.

Given the emphatic simplicity with which Magua and his followers are labelled as 'baddies', it is surprising that Fiedler is able to say with reference to Magua that 'the malice of the bad Indian demands as complicated a response as that of Shylock'. He takes his clue, as have other critics, from Shylock's words in *The Merchant of Venice* which are reproduced as an epigraph to this chapter: 'cursed be my tribe / If I forgive him!' From Cooper's own words in the chapter, however, it is surely clear that he regards Magua simply as a vindictive villain. One imagines that he alludes to Shylock, because he also regards Shakespeare's character in the same way. Certainly, the creation of Shylock and the presentation of racial issues in *The Merchant of Venice* are immensely more complex than anything in *The Last of the Mohicans*. Cooper can never give Magua anything like the lines: 'Hath not a Jew eyes? . . .'[15]

His association of Magua with Shylock, and also on occasions with Milton's Satan, belongs to the book's prevailing spirit of fancifulness and titillation. In this spirit, Cooper likes to get young women into helpless situations where, realistically, the only outcome would be rape. The spirit inspires him to thoughts of a sexually potent woman, Cora, in relationship with a male savage of equal potence. In so far as he is appalled by this relationship, the savage is Magua. When the relationship can be sublimated, Magua becomes Uncas. Even the favourable treatment of Indian life, however, is only an act of elegiac beguilement. By the end, Uncas and Magua have been killed off, and what is left of the Indians is of no moment, not even the Indian women's visionary song of Uncas's and Cora's union beyond the grave:

> The scout, to whom alone, of all the white men, the words were intelligible, suffered himself to be a little roused from his meditative posture . . . But when they spoke of the future prospects of Cora and Uncas, he shook his head, like one who knew the error of their simple creed . . . Happily for the self-command of both Heyward and Munro, they knew not the meaning of the wild sounds they heard.
>
> (Chapter 33)

Unlike George Dekker,[16] I find the scout's response here to be endorsed by Cooper, who himself implies that Heyward and

Munro would share the response, if they understood the meaning of 'the wild sounds they heard'. Dekker's argument joins with that of others who also want to separate Cooper from Hawk-eye. Donald Davie, for example, claims that in *The Last of the Mohicans* the scout is 'above all a bloodthirsty and superstitious figure, living by a code which the novelist disapproves of'.[17]

That Hawk-eye is 'bloodthirsty and superstitious' is certainly true. He leads an attack on enemy Indians with a cry which, if we have read *Heart of Darkness*, appalls: 'Extarminate the varlets! no quarter to an accursed Mingo'.[18] After this battle, we are told how 'the honest, but implacable scout, made the circuit of the dead, into whose senseless bosoms he thrust his long knife, with as much coolness, as though they had been as many brute carcasses!' (Chapter 12). On a later occasion, when Hawk-eye's party arrives at the aftermath of the massacre, he instructs Uncas to 'come away this way, lad, and let the raven settle upon the Mingo. I know, from seeing it, that they have a craving for the flesh of an Oneida' (Chapter 18).

Do such episodes reveal Cooper's disapproval of Hawk-eye? I think not. Immediately before Hawk-eye's stabbing of the dead bodies, when Magua has given Hawk-eye's party the slip, we read:

"Twas like himself!' cried the inveterate forester, whose pre-judices contributed so largely to veil his natural sense of justice in all matters which concerned the Mingoes; 'a lying and deceit-ful varlet as he is!'

(Chapter 12)

This view of Magua is Cooper's own. Hawk-eye's prejudices in this respect are also his creator's. *The Last of the Mohicans* is full of slurs against Indians (they are always so easy to fool), about which Cooper and Hawk-eye, as in the first paragraph of Chapter 24, are in complete accord. Cooper's indulgence of Hawk-eye is why the words, 'honest and implacable', in response to Hawk-eye's stab-bing of dead bodies, are a hopelessly evasive authorial comment on what the scout is doing. Contrast the author's emphatic con-demnation of Magua, none of whose deeds approaches Hawk-eye's ghoulishness.

It is true, as Davie argues, that Natty Bumppo is not always the same character from Tale to Tale. Since Cooper never takes an overview of the character in all the Tales, we may well conclude his purposes from Tale to Tale are always momentary and casually unrelated. Another possibility would be to see the different Natty Bumppos as signalling Cooper's intuitive compulsion to put any one conception of the character under the critical pressure of another conception. Not only would Natty Bumppo be placed in a critical context in some individual Tales (especially against Judge Temple in *The Pioneers* and Ishmael Bush in *The Prairie*), he would also be placed in this context from Tale to Tale. What we get in *The Last of the Mohicans*, therefore, is the frontier war experience the sanctimonious and apparently guiltless figure in *The Pioneers* and *The Prairie* might well have been through. Cooper needs Natty Bumppo as a figure outside civilisation to voice criticisms of civilisation. He cannot, however, settle for any one version of him, no more than can Poe with Pym, Melville with Ishmael, Twain with Huck.

I would be more persuaded by this latter thesis if the unsettled characterisation of Natty were matched by a sense of Cooper being fundamentally disturbed, as are Poe, Melville and Twain, by the nature of life. What I repeatedly come back to in *The Leather-Stocking Tales* is how untroubled Cooper remains. In *The Last of the Mohicans* the massacre in Chapter 18, which in reality would have unhinged anyone who experienced it, is a mere passing event, presented without credibility. Cooper makes everything easy for himself by evading reality. Hawk-eye's final commitment to Chingachgook, therefore, is sentimental on both his and his creator's part, because nothing has been sacrificed on its behalf. It has cost nothing. Hawk-eye, after all, has begun with Chingachgook where Leatherstocking in *The Pioneers* left off. He tells the chief: 'There is reason in an Indian, though nature has made him with a red skin', and: 'You are a just man for an Indian' (Chapter 3).

IV

Cooper wants good Indian blood to contribute to the civilised, white American identity, but it is to be acquired by the adoption of an Indian name, not by interbreeding. In this respect, what we learn of Duncan Uncas Middleton in Chapter 10 of *The Prairie* repeats what we learned of the Effinghams at the end of *The Pioneers*. All the good blood of the New World flows in one white stream, and whatever blood has been shed never poisons the stream. As in the case of the Sioux Indians in *The Prairie*, it was bad and treacherous blood anyway, needing to be eradicated. Bad Indians can be killed. Good Indians, meanwhile, even after a victory over bad Indians, consent to their own eventual dispossession by whites:

> The victors seemed to have lost every trace of ferocity with their success, and appeared disposed to consult the most trifling of the wants of that engrossing people who were daily encroaching on their rights, and reducing the Redmen of the west from their state of proud independence to the condition of fugitives and wanderers.
>
> (Chapter 33[19])

The irony here suggests Cooper himself can hardly believe what he claims is happening. Such doubt as he has, however, is never allowed to be troublesome. By the end of *The Prairie*, the whites, 'that engrossing people', have done very well indeed, and Cooper can write the kind of ending James was to mock in 'The Art of Fiction' (1884): 'a distribution at the last of prizes, pensions, husbands, wives, babies, millions, appended paragraphs, and cheerful remarks'. It is the ending no other American writer in this book could envisage.

The best moments in *The Prairie* relate to the tension between Ishmael Bush and Natty Bumppo, who is now, ten years after *The Pioneers*, the aged 'trapper'. The characterisation of Bush is Cooper's most challenging critique of the ideal he presented in Natty. In *The Prairie*, Natty bears more resemblance to the original Leatherstocking of *The Pioneers* than to the Hawk-eye of *The Last of the Mohicans*. The ennobling account of the trapper in Chapter 10 of *The Prairie*, even though it looks back to events in *The Last of the Mohicans*, pays no heed to the figure who in that book had methodically stabbed dead Indian bodies. As in *The Pioneers*, the trapper in *The Prairie* is a sort of magus in relationship to nature. A herd of rampaging buffaloes divides around him when he stands his ground in Chapter 19, and prairie fire responds to his control in Chapter 23.

'Dazzling and tremendous how quick the sunrise would kill me, / If I could not now and always send sunrise out of me.' In *The Prairie*, Cooper has something of Whitman's stark knowledge in these lines from poem 25 of 'Song of Myself'. The trapper's initial appearance amid the fiery light of the western sun makes the point of Whitman's second line. It is the American self in complete accord with the energy of the New World. The characterisation of Ishmael Bush, however, reminds us of Whitman's previous line:

> For the first time, in a life of much wild adventure, Ishmael felt a keen sense of solitude. The naked prairies began to assume the forms of illimitable and dreary wastes, and the rushing of the wind sounded like the whisperings of the dead.
>
> (Chapter 32)

With this awareness that the American scene can overwhelm, Cooper, as Nash Smith observes, 'suddenly moves into the consciousness'[20] of Ishmael Bush. From the beginning he has been intermittently fascinated by the character. When Bush is first described, his 'singular and wild display of prodigal and ill judged ornaments' (Chapter 1) suggests both a piratical nature, befitting someone with his contempt for the law, and also a desparate attempt to settle for something of value and even of personal enhancement. This attempt is random and incoherent, because there is no system to which Bush's accoutrements collectively belong. It reminds us that in the vast space of the New World, there is no authoritative reason to be anyone or anything.

Bush is the antithesis to the idealised thesis of Natty Bumppo. He provides a glimpse of the moral and spiritual destitution that might really await on the frontier, just as Pap Finn in *Huckleberry Finn* is a glimpse of what might really await on the run. Aside from this function, however, Bush is either involved in foolish adventures, or rendered lounging and immobile, so that Cooper will not have to think what to do with him.

The difference in *The Prairie*, from what Whitman and Twain offer, is that everyone eventually settles for conventional civilisation. With Bush initially as impatient of the law as Leatherstocking was in *The Pioneers* and performing therefore the out and out rebel function, the trapper in *The Prairie* can accept the value of the law. He dies, grasping Middleton as firmly as he grasps the good Indian, Hard-Heart. As for Bush, he finally returns to the settlements. At his moment of crisis over Abiram White, he had needed to turn to the Bible, the founding book of the settlements. Realistically, there is a truth in his conceding that the prairie is too much to be faced. Other nineteenth-century American writers

represent this moment too. Yet they continue to kick loose from
the settlements and to face the space again and again and again.

V

Cooper's return to Natty Bumppo in *The Pathfinder* (1840) and *The
Deerslayer* (1841) confirms that he never saw the character as a
radically challenging voice. All critical perspectives on the character, such as were provided by Judge Temple and Ishmael Bush, are
absent from these Tales. In the first of them, in which Natty is
nearly forty and called 'Pathfinder', we encounter the story of his
unrequited love for Mabel Dunham. That Natty Bumppo had
loved and lost might have cast a whole new light on his subsequent life. It might have qualified the apparent completeness of
that life by suggesting what had been missed by it. *The Pathfinder*,
however, presents nothing of this order. The love story only
complements the authorial sentimentalisation of Natty, evident in
passages of commentary on the character such as the one found in
Chapter 9.

Elsewhere, this novel involves Pathfinder in adventures in
which his relationship with Chingachgook is very peripheral. With
the other characters, Pathfinder is manipulated into unbelievable
situations, so that Cooper can present a clarification and a rescue.
An example of what I mean is the incredible notion that the so
obviously open-hearted Jasper Western could ever be so successfully maligned that, even by his closest friends, he is thought to be
a French spy.

VI

In the last sentence of *The Deerslayer* Cooper concludes:

> We live in a world of transgressions and selfishness, and no
> pictures that represent us otherwise can be true, though, hap-
> pily for human nature, gleamings of that pure spirit in whose
> likeness man has been fashioned are to be seen, relieving its
> deformities and mitigating if not excusing its crimes.[21]

In this final Tale it is in the twenty-year-old Natty, now called

Deerslayer, that we find 'gleamings of that pure spirit in whose likeness man has been fashioned'. Earlier in the novel, Deerslayer has recalled a line from 'The Lord's Prayer': 'God's will be done, on 'earth as it is in heaven' (Chapter 28). For Cooper, his whole life is now an expression of a kind of New Testament Christianity, in so far as Christian beliefs can be exemplified in the adventures created for him.

These centre on Deerslayer's and Chingachgook's first warpath. When we meet Deerslayer initially, he has not yet killed his man. He does so, with appropriate chivalry, in Chapter 7, a chapter of very good reportage which certainly earns a claim to being, in Winters' words, 'probably' 'the best single passage of prose in Cooper'.[22]

Not that this momentous event signifies any development or change in Deerslayer. Throughout the book he remains the monotonous representation of an authorial idea. When he himself is not moralising, his creator (for example, in Chapters 12, 24 and 26) is moralising about him in the manner which began in *The Pathfinder*. Deerslayer might well grow up into Pathfinder. Cooper's insistent claims for 'this extraordinary being' (Chapter 16), however, offer no overview of his subsequent life. Deerslayer's first killing of an Indian occasions no authorial reflection on his later bloodthirstiness in *The Last of the Mohicans*. His rejection of Judith Hutter as a wife provokes no comment on Mabel Dunham's forthcoming rejection of him as a husband.

The simple moralistic terms in which Judith herself is imagined by Cooper, and rejected by him as well as by Deerslayer, pervade the whole book. Before the arrival of Deerslayer in her life, Judith has been all coquetry and vanity. Army officers flirt with her, but for respectability's sake she may well have to become the wife of someone like the boisterous, patronising and morally stupid Henry March ('Hurry Harry'). This threadbare conception precludes the possibility that some man, even an officer, might genuinely fall in love with a beautiful and spirited woman. Instead, Judith is required by Cooper to abase herself and seek redemption from her sense of her fallen state by trying to become Deerslayer's wife. His very presence reveals other men in her experience to be worthless.

Rejected by Deerslayer, Judith's fate is sealed, and, in the novel's last paragraph, she is back in England as the mistress of Sir Robert Warley. *The Deerslayer*, therefore, is an exception among the Leather-

Stocking Tales in that it does not have Cooper's usual 'white', civilised ending, expressed in a reconciling marriage. As the novel's final sentence indicates, its world is one of 'transgression and selfishness'. The only exceptions to this view are Deerslayer, Chingachgook and his betrothed, and Judith's sister, Hetty, whose wits are enfeebled.

The concluding pronouncement undoubtedly confirms *The Deerslayer* as a more pessimistic book than the previous Tales. In it, the whites' incursion on the Indian and the wilderness is enacted by Hurry Harry and Judith's and Hetty's stepfather, Tom Hutter. Driven by cupidity and racism, these men's exploits have no redeeming feature. For money, they will scalp any Indian man, woman or child. They even try to scalp Chingachgook's wife, though the attempt, amazingly, occasions no indignation from the noble savage. Eventually, Tom Hutter is himself horribly scalped at the end of Chapter 20. He fittingly reaps what he sows.

Even such a powerful moment cannot rescue the simplicity of the book's thesis that, among white men, Deerslayer is good, the rest bad. It is true that Cooper warms to Hurry Harry's boisterous energy and can catch in Chapter 19, when the man has shot an Indian girl, a rare moment of self-questioning. These hints of complication, however, only serve to underline its general absence in a book which is over-long, and which has too many incidents requiring us to take an unrewarded leave of our senses.

That Cooper is left at the end of *The Leather-Stocking Tales* with only the young Natty Bumppo for consolation might have been interesting. It might have signified Cooper's final arrival in that state of unaccommodation in which the later writers in this book begin. The young Natty Bumppo in *The Deerslayer*, however, is already as an old man, his alleged age being no more than a piece of information to justify his adventures. Morally, he is already accommodated for life. Cooper has found without much search. The later writers search endlessly.

2

Poe's Fiction: *Arthur Gordon Pym* to 'The Black Cat'

I

Even though it is modelled on *Robinson Crusoe*, the American *Arthur Gordon Pym* undermines the English realism *Robinson Crusoe* helps to found, together with the assumptions of coherence which that realism expresses. The contrast between the two books is immediately apparent in their respective prefaces. In the 'Preface' to the English work, we meet an editor who assures us of the truth of what the narrator will subsequently relate. Such an opening manoeuvre was to become in many later novels a standard way of presenting fiction as, in the words of *Robinson Crusoe*'s 'Preface', 'a just history of fact'. Even though the fact were fiction, it was reported as a reality which affirmed the real world presumed to be inhabited by author and reader.

Arthur Gordon Pym's 'Preface' parodies *Robinson Crusoe*'s by having its narrator (allegedly Pym) introduce its editor (allegedly Poe). This reversal of the usual introductory procedure is elaborated by the teasing claim that the first few pages of the succeeding narrative were written as a trial run by 'Mr Poe'. According to the 'Preface', it was thought that coming from Mr Poe's pen such pages could only be read as fiction. It was when the pages from Mr Poe were surprisingly given credence, that Pym was persuaded he himself could write his story and also be believed.

Arthur Gordon Pym's 'Preface' is a joke about the joke of fiction pretending to be fact. In it Pym gives life to Poe, who in his turn will give death to Pym in the matching 'Note' after the narrative has finished. Despite *Arthur Gordon Pym*'s resemblance to *Robinson Crusoe* in its authenticity of detail, it is always recognised in the American work that author and narrator have created each other in a world of fiction. In this respect, they are like Melville and

Ishmael in *Moby Dick*, Twain and Huck in *Huckleberry Finn*; indeed Huck in his opening words also introduces 'Mr Mark Twain'. All is fiction to the extent that in the American context there is no objective structure of reality to be imitated. I am aware that Coleridge's 'The Rime of the Ancyent Marinere' (1798) comes between *Robinson Crusoe* and *Arthur Gordon Pym*, and that the fantastic adventures at sea in the English poem contribute to the fantastic adventures at sea in Poe's story. It can be argued that in the body of Coleridge's baffling poem we have an example of an English work which likewise finds no congruence with a reality outside itself. Yet the Ancyent Marinere does get himself back to civilisation, where it seems he has something of an ongoing life telling his story. For audience he has 'the wedding-guest', who, like the presumed audience outside the poem, is living a recognisably actual life. In these ways, 'The Rime of the Ancyent Marinere' manages to retain a foothold in reality.

There is no such resting place for *Arthur Gordon Pym*. Accordingly, the identity and function of its narrator, as is the case with Melville's Ishmael and Twain's Huck, serve only the immediate needs of the fiction. Even the slightest implication that the narrator has an ongoing life in an actual world cannot be sustained, since the fiction will require him to be a creature of radical inconsistencies:

> I warmly pressed upon him the expediency of persevering, at least for a few days longer, in the direction we were now holding. So tempting an opportunity of solving the great problem in regard to an Antarctic continent had never yet been afforded to man, and I confess that I felt myself bursting with indignation at the timid and ill-timed suggestions of our commander.
>
> (Chapter 17[1])

This Pym, who towards the end of the narrative has such influence and such knowledge about the problem of the Antarctic, bears no consistent relation to the adolescent and easily-led Pym who began the narrative.

Similarly, the various parts of *Arthur Gordon Pym* have no developing relationship in terms of time. As in *Moby Dick* and *Huckleberry Finn*, the only time is the present time of any particular episode in the fiction. This 'present' exists without reference to remembered experiences and structures of the past, or anticipated experiences and structures of the future. Time in *Arthur Gordon Pym* is as it is in Pym's log – no more than succession. I recognise that time is also a notorious problem in *Robinson Crusoe*. In this case, however, the problem is to do with Defoe's inability to represent what might be the developing psychological and physical condition of someone on the island for twenty-eight years. Rudimentary as it is, the incremental, 'what comes next' structure of *Robinson Crusoe* expresses certainty rather than uncertainty. Crusoe lives in a world which he and his readers confidently possess. Whenever doubts occur, as when Crusoe is ill and has a terrible dream, there is always access to a divine scheme of things. Pym's world, by contrast, offers no intimations of such coherence. If his own intermittent genuflections to God do remind us of Crusoe's, it is because they are Crusoe's. Fiction parodying fiction, they are no more than momentary imports from Defoe's book.

Since the objective world and the subjective self are mutually reflective, a plotless world entails the disintegration of the self. In this condition of disintegration, Pym predicts many of the voices of nineteenth-century American literature with their insistent, unanswerable question: 'What shall we call our "self"? Where does it begin? Where does it end?'[2] The daylight world of reason in *Arthur Gordon Pym* is undermined by underground worlds of delirium, hallucination, incoherence, madness. The conscious self is betrayed by the body's diseases and eventual putrefaction, the corpse of an Augustus becoming 'loathsome beyond expression, and so far decayed that, as Peters attempted to lift it, an entire leg came off in his grasp' (Chapter 13). Encompassing all is a world of mutiny, cannibalism and terrible appetence:

At this instant another sudden yaw brought the region of the forecastle for a moment into view, and we beheld at once the origin of the sound. We saw the tall stout figure still leaning on the bulwark, and still nodding his head to and fro, but his face was now turned from us so that we could not behold it. His arms were extended over the rail, and the palms of his hands fell outward. His knees were lodged upon a stout rope, tightly stretched, and reaching from the heel of the bowsprit to a cathead. On his back, from which a portion of the shirt had been torn, leaving it bare, there sat a huge seagull, busily gorging itself with the horrible flesh, its bill and tallons deep buried, and its white plumage spattered all over with blood.

(Chapter 10)

In 'The Ancyent Marinere' continuing original sin is committed by the mariner against the albatross. Here we have the reverse: atrocity committed on the body of man, even as he is in the position of imploring prayer to the wide, wide sea. Similarly, the orderly, Defoe-like observation of detail in the above passage undermines, by what it records, the assumed coherence such observation is meant to serve.

The racial antipathies in *Arthur Gordon Pym* surely belong to the book's overall sense of life's irreconcilable polarities and conflicts, and not entirely, as Harry Levin has argued influentially,[3] to racial prejudice on the part of Poe the Southerner. In the reporting of the experience of Pym and his companions in the world of the Tsalalians, I am reminded often of the ambivalence of tone to be found also in Melville's *Typee* (1846) and Twain's *A Connecticut Yankee at King Arthur's Court* (1889). In all three books we have a disturbed, unaccommodated American consciousness, unconvinced that worlds are ever new, and mindful from national experience of the inevitable violence and slaughter resulting from any one world's incursion on another.

What remains after such knowledge but 'that American humour' cited by James as the sole consolation for his compatriots' terrible state of 'denudation'?[4] Here, James is referring (humorously) to the lack of co-ordinates for understanding American experience. If humour were not a response to this denudation, madness, encountered often in Poe, might be. For its part *Arthur Gordon Pym*, which began with the joke of its 'Preface', ends with the joke of its 'Note', resting in the uninterpretable by parodying interpretation. Towards the end of the narrative, original or ultimate chasms have been explored and original or ultimate hieroglyphs discovered. Chasms and hieroglyphs are reproduced as signs, but to what structure of meaning do the signs belong? It is the continuing question of American literature. That it may find no answer from the traditional structures of the English language is confirmed by the 'Ethiopian', 'Arabic' and 'Egyptian' verbal traces Poe has recourse to. He is joking, but he is also serious.

II

We leave Pym to his American fate, facing the blank unknown with the structures of the Old World left behind. Poe's New World point of view attests in story after story to the disintegration of Old World coherences, even as they have reached a high point of development and sophistication. As Lawrence puts it at the beginning of his essay on Poe: he 'is absolutely concerned with the disintegration-process of his own psyche . . . a disintegrating and sloughing of the old consciousness'.[5] So, in 'The Masque of the Red Death' (1842), Prospero's representative Old World domain is destroyed by plague and death, against which the elaborate resources of its culture provide no security. Similarly in 'Ligeia' (1838), the eponymous heroine is utterly unsustained by the immensity of her learning from the past. In her poem (added to the text in 1845), life is 'much of Madness and more of Sin, / And Horror the soul of the plot'.[6] As in *Arthur Gordon Pym*, incoherence outside the self is mirrored by incoherence within the self: Ligeia is 'the most violently a prey to the tumultuous vultures of stern passion'. From all her accumulated wisdom, only the fragment from Glanvill celebrating the 'will'[7] gives Ligeia any expectation that meaningless life will not be followed by meaningless death.

At her death, the narrator, for whom Ligeia was as a sublime muse proffering transcendence, is left without purpose. His decoration of his abbey in England is the expression of an imagination at its last abberrant and extravagant gasp. As represented by its artefacts, culture here has become no more than booty. One thinks of James's similar understanding of terminal conditions in, say, *The Spoils of Poynton* (1897), *The Wings of the Dove* (1902) and *The Golden Bowl* (1904). In such a context people prey on one another, unsustained and unrestrained by the veneer of manners. Fundamental passions and wills surface. So the dark-haired Kate Croy, 'the panther', preys on the red-haired Milly Theale, 'the dove', in *The Wings of the Dove*. In Poe, admittedly, we have nothing like James's social realism, attenuated as that realism in the later novelist is. It may be that 'Ligeia' and several other Poe stories exist only as fantasies within the narrator's self-expressing consciousness. Even so, we have irreconcilable polarisation between Ligeia, the dark principle of life, and Rowena, the light principle of life. In such a state of anarchy, the Glanvill pronouncement is clutched as a last cultural straw in the wind. It becomes, as such things will in these circumstances, both a talisman against the void and also a triumphant slogan justifying an act of extermination.

'The Fall of the House of Usher' (1839) presents in Usher himself a consciousness poised at the point of the collapse of Old World orders. The poem in the middle of the story dramatises the mythical background to the state of affairs we encounter. It recounts the falling apart of a harmonious, hierarchical order in which art was:

> A troop of Echoes whose sweet duty
>   Was but to sing,
> In voices of surpassing beauty,
>   The wit and wisdom of their king.

It is true that the Eden-like imperium of culture presented in the poem cannot without qualification be claimed to represent the Old World. The poem evokes a mythical, harmonious past to which any actual world, amid all its conflicts, might nostalgically look back. Nonetheless, it can be argued that much art in the Old World is, as in the poem, an echo and a mirror-image of that world's hierarchy. 'The Fall of the House of Usher' is itself evidence for this argument. In its formal manner of narration, in the ancient house and family surrounded by the peasantry, and in the leisured and cultivated life (such as it is presented) at the house, the story adopts its very being from an Old World order.

As an American story, however, it represents this order as played out. The implicit question is what will follow. At the end of *Nature* (1836), Emerson answers this question for his compatriots with the injunction: 'Build, therefore, your own world'. Whitman complies and when, as in 'Song of Myself', he can affect his most confident voice, he creates for the self the new, outgoing, democratic world of America. For Poe, by contrast, 'Build, therefore, your own world' results, as in the case of Usher, in the self turning relentlessly inward, becoming self-imprisoning, solipsistic and murderous. Against its ruins, it too, like the consciousness in 'Ligeia' and in Eliot's *The Waste Land* (1922), can provide only remote fragments of culture, exemplified in 'the books which, for years, had formed no small portion of the mental existence of the invalid'. Its terminal and unrestrained condition produces, as in *The Waste Land*, a 'perversion and amplification' of the art of others, while its own creativity is expressed in 'pure abstractions' and 'phantasmagoric conceptions'. None of these resources relieves Usher of his subjugation to 'some fatal demon of fear'.

Poised at the end of things, with himself and a New World to create, Usher is a prototype of the estranged consciousness we find not only in Eliot but also in Hawthorne, Dickinson and James. This consciousness moreover is at least implicit in Whitman, Melville, Twain and Faulkner, despite the manifest actuality of the worlds these authors present. Amid the disintegration of society's order, Usher is the artist as hero, seeking a transcendent life of the imagination. For Poe, the creation of Usher is very much an act of self-examination. Like Usher's, Poe's own art is often parasitic, abstract and phantasmagoric. This very story, even as it affects Old World manners, is moving away from any notion of realism these manners imply to a world entirely of the imagination. Like many of Poe's poems (especially 'The Raven' (1845) and 'Ulalume' (1847)), and like many other Poe stories, this work will not let us forget that it is artifice. In so far as it seeks validation, it does so not by reference to a world which might be believed to exist outside of itself, but by reference to other books. Some of these are 'real', or, in the case of 'The Mad Trist', 'unreal', though 'The Mad Trist' becomes as real as any other work of literature (a typically provocative manoeuvre by Poe) in so far as Poe writes it within the story. We have entered, that is, a world of words which, unlike such examples of English Gothic fiction as *The Mysteries of Udolpho* (1794) and *Frankenstein* (1818), retains no foothold in a reality outside of itself. As is usually the case in Poe, we do not know from where the narrator walks into the story, nor to where the narrator flees out of the story.

Whatever else is meant by the relationship between Usher and Madeline, it is clear that this affair also signifies Usher's attempt to transcend materiality, even the materiality of the self. As his twin, with 'figure', 'air' and 'features' identical to his, Madeline from birth must have seemed to Usher barely other than himself. For Usher to hurry on Madeline's death by entombing her living body, therefore, is in effect to entomb, and achieve release from, his own material body. A restored, solitary Adam, Usher would then have built his own world in a manner and with a result unimagined by Emerson, Thoreau and Whitman. He would be a free spirit, untouchable by materiality and death. The absoluteness of the imagination would be guaranteed.

Mark Kinkead-Weekes has pointed out that Madeline recalls the

Magdelen, 'the archetype of the refining of the fleshly into saint-liness'.[8] Roderick Usher, therefore, like several other male figures in Poe (for example, the narrator of 'Ligeia' and the voice of the poem 'To Helen' (1831)), is one more tormented Adam of the American imagination, annihilating the female body in order to sublimate the female spirit and thereby achieve his own male sublimation. I am seeing him as the expression of a New World spirit, desiring to break free of the decay of the Old World and longing for transcendence. In the event, inescapable materiality and mortality 'comes back', as Melville is to put it when he too is seeking transcendence, 'in horror'.[9] Madeline, like Hester Prynne, has been wasted by male vengeance, but, also like Hester, she will never be submissive. With 'blood upon her white robes, and evidence of some bitter struggle upon every portion of her ema-ciated frame', she returns to fall upon her brother in what Kinkead-Weekes rightly sees as a perverted parody of the sexual act. In this story, as in several nineteenth-century American works, there will be no fruitful intercourse between the self and otherness. For characters and author the end is oblivion.

III

Not surprisingly, when Poe offers us something approaching a realistic social world, as in 'William Wilson' (1839) and 'The Man of the Crowd' (1840), the significance lies not in the presentation of that world for itself, but in Poe's interest in individual states of estrangement within it. Mabbott, the editor of the *Collected Works*, establishes Dickens's influence on 'The Man of the Crowd'. This connection with the English writer, however, only serves to show how comparatively lifeless Poe's presentation of London scenes in this story is. Poe is never very good when he needs to represent an actual social world as distinct from a mainly symbolic world. 'William Wilson' suffers in this respect. First of all, the parapher-nalia to do with the school in England is indulged entirely for its own sake. Secondly, Poe cannot imagine for his narrator a life which would justify the claims of turpitude made for it. Instead we get verbal filler, for example: 'Let it suffice, that among spend-thrifts I out-Heroded Herod.'

Such is the failure of even the famous Dupin stories to present its characters as part of a world of any actual substance, that these

stories remain at best momentary entertainments, set up to illustrate their theory of Dupin's superior ratiocinative powers. They
are the work of a Poe who, as in 'The Gold Bug' (1843), enjoyed
posing and solving puzzles for their own sake. 'Oedipus, Hamlet
and Dupin each epitomize an ideological moment', claims Robert
Giddings.[10] Dupin's involvements, however, are too insignificant
to justify placing the character in this kind of company. 'The
Murders of the Rue Morgue' (1841), if only because of what is
implied by Dupin's solution of the crime, is the most rewarding of
his stories, although it is too long for what it offers as a whole. In
the story Dupin's rationality, in all its supremacy, leads, as we
might now expect from Poe, only to the non-rational, the murderous orang-utan. As is frequently the case in nineteenth-century
American literature, thesis meets head-on the antithesis which
cancels it out.

Not that 'William Wilson' and especially 'The Man of the Crowd'
do not survive their realistic shortcomings. Both exemplify Poe's
repeated and frequently noticed obsession with characters who
double each other. This obsession replaces an interest in other
figures for their own sake and precludes, therefore, an interest in a
realistic social world. It is a fascination we also find in the other
American writers in this book. In nineteenth-century American
literature, the self is rarely settled, rarely part of a social and
historical context in which it may feel established. It has to be
repeatedly reaffirmed, often, as in 'William Wilson', against rival
energies within the self. 'The Soul selects her own Society – / Then
– shuts the Door –', writes Dickinson in poem 303. So too, in 'The
Cask of Amontillado' (1846), the Fortunato of the self if walled up,
in order that another self may try to live.

Not even in European settings can Poe's American imagination
find settlement for the self. In this respect, Poe anticipates James.
The motto of 'The Man of the Crowd' reads in translation: 'That
great evil, to be unable to be alone'. Yet the old man in the story,
the representative human self at the end of its life, cannot but be
alone, since the evil which compels him to seek relief from the self
is also the evil which forever prevents him reaching out from the
self. Essentially, his case has universal significance, taking me as
far back as the wandering and despairing old man in Chaucer's
'The Pardoner's Tale'. In the American context, as we read the first
paragraph of the story we surely think of Hawthorne's 'The Minister's Black Veil' (1836) and of Dimmesdale in *The Scarlet Letter*:

There are some secrets which do not permit themselves to be told. Men die nightly in their beds, wringing the hands of ghostly confessors, and looking them piteously in the eyes – die with despair of heart and convulsion of throat, on account of the hideousness of mysteries which will not *suffer themselves* to be revealed. Now and then, alas, the conscience of man takes up a burden so heavy in horror that it can be thrown down only in the grave. And thus the essence of all crime is undivulged.

In the ensuing story the old man is alone in a crowded city, a setting Hawthorne does not present. He is as alone as the 'I' and the old knife-grinder in Whitman's 'Sparkles from the Wheel' (1871), as alone as the figures and voices in the 'Unreal City' of *The Waste Land*. The implication is that every individual of the crowd will eventually be left thus, unsustained by whatever it is (if it is anything) that gives the ceaseless life of the city its meaning. The old man is likened to 'the fiend', because he unnervingly gives the lie to the city's surface conviviality and seeming collective purpose. 'The type and genius of deep crime', he is both of the city and against it. He is the individual calling in the city for a personal attention which the city with its intrinsic impersonality, can never give. I see the heartless London of Conrad's *The Secret Agent* (1907) here. I also see, as in several other Poe stories, a genesis of Conrad's use of his narrator, Marlow. The relationship of the narrator of 'The Man of the Crowd' to the old man, who is a potential self for the narrator, is the relationship of Marlowe to Kurtz in *Heart of Darkness* (1902). As he begins the story, Poe's narrator is recovering from an illness. He is ready to take up life anew. By the end, however, he is 'wearied unto death'. His encounter with the void at the heart of things leaves him, as Marlowe is left, spent and purposeless.

What is it, Poe is asking the reader, that sustains you in this life but remains unfound in my stories by my narrators and the figures who are their doubles? In 'The Tell-Tale Heart' (1843), 'The Black Cat' (1843) and 'The Imp of the Perverse' (1845), the question has a more disturbing particularity. 'Why *will* you say that I am mad?' the narrator of the first of these, who can represent all three narrators, asks us challengingly. In other words, 'If I'm mad, what's your sanity?'

The three stories confirm the essentially metaphysical nature of

Poe's work, which will eventually compel him to write *Eureka* (1848). By metaphysical, I mean to indicate that Poe's quest has always been to find what meaning, if any, there is to life, death and eternity. Another bald way of putting this is to say that he is trying to decide whether or not there is a God and, if there is, what purpose now and hereafter God has for humanity and the world. In both 'The Tell-Tale Heart' and 'The Imp of the Perverse' we find fragments from *Macbeth*, and I do not think it is going too far to build a little on these very slight connections. '[Life] is a tale / Told by an idiot . . . / Signifying nothing'[11] are Macbeth's well known words towards the end of the play. For Poe, in 'The Tell-Tale Heart', 'The Black Cat' and 'The Imp of the Perverse', the question is whether life is but a tale told by a madman signifying nothing.

Like other Poe narrators, the narrator of the first of these tales is profoundly disturbed (as who is not?) by the thought of mortality as the terrifying confirmation of life's impotence and insignificance. In 'The Colloquy of Monos and Una' (1841) which takes place in eternity, Una speaks for most of Poe's figures with these words: 'Ah, Death, the spectre which sate at all feasts! . . . How mysteriously did it act as a check to human bliss – saying unto it "thus far, and no further!"' The old man, the narrator's victim in 'The Tell-Tale Heart', predicts the narrator himself, carried that much nearer to death merely by ageing. The old man's 'eye of a vulture' can be seen as the eye of ravenous death fixed expectantly on the narrator. Thus the old man is the cause of an effect on the narrator. Reverse this thesis, however, and it is the narrator who is the cause of an effect on the old man. It is the narrator who is as death coming for the old man, pushing the old man into the grave by the inevitability of his younger, growing claim on life. The two are indeed agonised mirror images of each other and tormentingly complicitous in each other. This is why the narrator can say of someone he is about to murder: 'I loved the old man.' It is why he has such deep fellow feeling for him:

He was still sitting up in the bed listening; – just as I have done, night after night, hearkening to the death watches in the wall.
    Presently I heard a slight groan, and I knew it was the groan of mortal terror. It was not a groan of pain or of grief – oh, no! – it was the low stifled sound that arises from the bottom of the soul when overcharged with awe. I knew the sound well. Many a

night, just at midnight, when all the world slept, it has welled up from my bosom, deepening with its dreadful echo, the terrors that distracted me.

By colluding with what he grandiloquently alludes to as 'Death' and murdering the old man, the narrator seeks to transcend feelings of impotence,. terror and dread arising from the knowledge of his own mortality. He seeks absolution from the 'Evil Eye' of death he sees in the old man. He will be the agent of 'Death', a personified force, rather than a mere victim of death as an impersonal process. 'Never before that night', he tells us, 'had I *felt* the extent of my own powers.' As he enters the old man's bedchamber, he directs the ray of his lantern 'as if by instinct, precisely upon the damned spot'. He is referring to the old man's eye, but the phrase, 'damned spot', from *Macbeth* reminds us of the play, where it signifies the blood of the murdered Duncan which the deranged Lady Macbeth imagines she cannot wash from her hands. *Macbeth*, we might also remember, is a play in which Macbeth and Lady Macbeth themselves attempt to achieve transcendence and absoluteness ('that but this blow / Might be the be-all and the end-all' (I.vii. 4–5)) by murdering an old man. In the play the 'damned spot' is imagined to be on the hands of a perpetrator. In the story it is imagined as the eye of the victim. This transference is, I think, justified by the fact that in both play and story perpetrator becomes victim, just as victim has been perpetrator. At the beginning of the play, Duncan has acclaimed Macbeth's bloodiest acts of slaughter, while the old man with the 'eye of the vulture' is obsessively seen by the narrator as a perpetrating force.

I am not attempting to put 'The Tell-Tale Heart' on a par with *Macbeth*. The play unquestionably has a stature greater than anything Poe ever achieves. It is worth noting, however, that the premise richly inherited by Shakespeare (even if Shakespeare leaves the premise as unconfirmed as he found it), that there may be a major scale of significance to life and death, was *not* inherited by Poe. Poe is an American writer facing ultimate questions with little to go on that is relevant to where he is. If the phrases 'damned spot' in 'The Tell-Tale Heart' and 'trumpet-tongued' (I.vii. 19) in 'The Imp of the Perverse' strike us as preposterous borrowings from *Macbeth*, we should recognise that they are in part intended to. Like the mutilation of Hamlet's soliloquy ('the most celebrated thing in Shakespeare') in Chapter 21 of *Huckleberry Finn*, they function to deconstruct the context of significance available to Shakespeare in order to *con*struct whatever context of significance might be available to an American writer. That Shakespeare, if he were not treated with some irreverence, could be as much an incubus as an inspiration to an American writer is amply demon-strated in *Moby-Dick* and especially in *Pierre* (1852).

The momentariness and instantaneousness of Poe's stories, together with their stark polarisation of complicated issues, testify to the paucity of context he was able to find and create for himself. Often his stories are saved from their tendency towards abstraction (as, for example, 'The Domain of Arnheim' (1846) is not) by little more than the dramatic, soliloquising voices of the narrators. For Poe and his narrators it may be that life only is to be understood fleetingly as mad, or absurd, or perverse. Among the many works Poe's stories look forward to, as Harry Levin saw thirty years ago,[12] is Dostoyevsky's *Notes from Underground* (1864). Especially in the three stories presently under consideration, Poe's narrators may be unconsciously where Dostoyevsky's narrator (again in a richer context) is consciously, when he claims: 'I invented a life, so that I should at any rate *live*.'[13] Read in this way the stories have all the unreliable assertiveness ('I loved the old man'!) of those who desperately confess in order to claim a status for the self. Alterna-tively, the stories may be the unevoked, upwelling nightmares of lives unsustained by any structures that can even begin to pass as objective.

'Oh God! what *could* I do?' 'Almighty God! – no, no!' Is there a God to listen to these entreaties in the penultimate paragraph of 'The Tell-Tale Heart'? If there is, will an act of murder force God to reveal his hand? The whole story is an attempt to discover what moral terms, if any, life and death have. Phrases such as 'damned spot', 'Evil Eye' and 'hideous heart' seem to belong to no moral scheme. They indicate rather the betrayal of life by death, the heart being 'hideous', not because it is morally corrupt, but because it beats onward only towards the grave. No transcendence is achieved. Had he not confessed, it seems that even as a murderer the narrator would have lived insignificantly towards death.

In 'The Black Cat' the narrator tries to tell why he killed the animal which gives its name to the story:

> . . . hung it *because* I knew that in so doing I was committing a
> sin – a deadly sin that would so jeopardise my immortal soul as

to place it – if such a thing were possible – even beyond the reach of the infinite mercy of the Most Merciful and Most Terrible God.

Yet what can the narrator's 'immortal soul' and 'the infinite mercy of the Most Merciful and Most Terrible God' have to do with the life and death of cats, billions of which have been drowned at birth since time immemorial? In this story I think initially of Poe as metaphysical in the same way as Donne is. In Donne's poems, as is well known, seemingly unrelated ideas, energies and states of being are brought together so as to be mutually qualifying. With reference to 'The Black Cat' I am reminded especially of the poem, 'The Flea', in which an implicit question is: if a flea's activities and life are worth nothing, whose activities and life are worth anything?

The voice of 'The Flea', however, in all the extremities of its wit, is more anchored in a real and conventional world than ever Poe's narrator is in 'The Black Cat'. Whereas Donne's poem may negotiate a change in the meaning of words for our actual life, Poe's story leaves words unnegotiable and finally emptied of all meaning. It is typically American of him that in this respect he finds no accommodating reality in which to rest. Either the above quotation about hanging the cat refers to some scheme of life and death which makes sense, or language, like life, is a game we must play without knowing the rules. Does the cat's name, 'Pluto', mean anything (and for whom?), or was it chosen simply because someone liked the sound of it? The whole story is full of teases which are nonetheless desperate, because the narrator, as in a nightmare, believes he has committed atrocities but cannot understand why. Like so many nineteenth-century American fictional voices, not even from the ultimate end ('tomorrow I die') can he make sense. His terms collide and cancel one another out. We have on the one hand 'mere *Man*', whose 'paltry friendship and gossamer fidelity' is worth less than 'the unselfish and self-sacrificing love of a brute'. On the other hand we have man 'fashioned in the image of the High God'. Everything humanity does in the story questions this last proposition, or the image of God, or both.

IV

Poe has little, if anything, to say about the day-to-day personal, social and moral questions of our lives. Not even the remarkable adventure story, 'A Descent into the Maelstrom' (1841) refutes this statement. In this story it could be argued that there is something to be learned from the fisherman, the second narrator. It could be claimed that he earns his reprieve from the Maelstrom not only because of his powers of observation and calculation (powers valued by Poe in a number of stories), but also because of his selfless concern for his brother. Yet the first narrator of the story soon disappears from it and remains unlocatable. It is as if he has all along been recalling from another world a story which can have no relevance to wherever he is now, and which, therefore, leaves him unchanged. One more reason why Poe is limited to the short piece, or, as in *Arthur Gordon Pym*, to a longer piece of separable episodes, is that there is no possibility in his works of anyone or anything developing. All is fixed in its condition of being. Such an absence of potential makes a novel difficult, if not impossible, to do.

Poe is the American consciousness poised at an end, rather than at a beginning. America signifies that the Old World is finished, but Poe is not interested in what comes next, that is, in what America might offer as an actual, New World. 'The Colloquy of Monos and Una' and 'Mellonta Tauta' (1849) provide ample evidence of his disbelief in any advancement of the human condition to be expected from republican and democratic ideals.

The New World he desired was a transcendent world of the spirit which, unlike Emerson's, Thoreau's and Whitman's, proclaimed no material counterpart. Celebrated and theorised about in *Eureka*, it is the world to which all his narrators, from their condition of spiritual alienation, aspire. It is the world after the end, when 'the act of Creation has long ago ceased' (p. 271).[14] All will then return to '*Unity. This* is their lost parent' (p. 238). The universe will then be revealed as 'a plot of God' (p. 292), in which all causes which are also effects and all effects which are also causes will be reconciled. 'All being *Now*' (p. 264) with God, there will then be neither past nor future.

By the closing pages of *Eureka*, this vision in its spiritual rewards is hardly different from the Emersonian Transcendentalism Poe habitually scorned. Like Transcendentalism, it is an attempt to fill the space of America with meaning – such meaning as Poe's narrators were in despair of ever finding.

3

Hawthorne: *The Scarlet Letter* (1850)

In contrast to other American writers in this book, whose first person forms capture instants of time unrelated to any other time, Hawthorne narrates *The Scarlet Letter* as a third person, historical novelist, looking back from the present to the past. This historian's role seems to be the same as Scott's in *The Heart of Midlothian* (1818).[1] In the 'Custom-House' prologue to *The Scarlet Letter* Hawthorne claims, as does Scott in the preliminaries to his novel, that what we are to read is not fiction, but history derived from discovered evidence. He goes on to declare himself no more than the 'editor' of the story that is to follow.

This story is immediately remarkable for its vivid presentation of life in seventeenth-century Boston, 'a little town on the edge of the western wilderness' (Chapter 2).[2] Hawthorne convinces us he has captured the collective mind and spirit of 'a people among whom religion and law were almost identical' (Chapter 2), a community 'accomplishing so much precisely because it imagined and hoped so little' (Chapter 3). As in these quotations, Hawthorne's expository prose has all the more authority because of the critical objectivity which tempers his inwardness with the early settlers' situation.

The historical form gave him perspective, a perspective as much on the present as on the past. For Hawthorne the sense of history had everything to do with immediate questions of personal and national identity. As he tells us in 'The Custom-House', he himself looked back 'two centuries and a quarter' to the 'original Briton, the earliest emigrant of my name'. In his case, his own family had been so long settled in Salem that for a time he 'felt it almost as a destiny to make Salem my home'. From this past, moreover, Hawthorne was able to inherit all the significance of an identity which was tormented and guilty. In their day his ancestors had persecuted Quakers and witches. As their heir, Hawthorne took 'shame upon myself for their sakes, and [prayed] that any curse incurred by them . . . may be now and henceforth removed'.

'Few of my countrymen', Hawthorne acknowledged, could know what this sense of history was. It was the very sense Emerson, Thoreau and Whitman sought to annul. Emerson is expressing its antithesis in Chapter 6 of *Nature* (1836), when he defines Idealism:

> Idealism sees the world in God. It beholds the whole circle of persons and things, of actions and events, of country and religion, not as painfully accumulated, atom after atom, act after act, in an aged creeping Past, but as one vast picture, which God paints on the instant eternity for the contemplation of the soul.

This passage is only one example of Emerson's frequent use of the metaphor of the circle to express the meaning of life. In the first paragraph of his essay 'Circles' (1840) he tells us: 'St Augustine described the nature of God as a circle whose centre was everywhere and its circumference nowhere.' Like his followers, Thoreau and Whitman, Emerson wanted to free Americans especially from history's long and corrupt chain of cause and effect, from 'an aged creeping Past', beginning with the Fall. Eternity or History would be conceived not in linear but in circular terms. An individual soul, an individual nation, could at any moment in time be at the centre and at one with the source of all creation. The New World, therefore, was always as near as was the Old World to Genesis. It was not overshadowed by the corrupt past of the Old World, but, in Whitman's phrase in poem 1 of 'Song of Myself', could speak uncompromised 'with original energy'. There could be, as Emerson puts it, 'instant eternity', original communion with God.

Such was the faith Hawthorne must have experienced during his stay in 1841 with the Transcendental commune at Brook Farm. In 'The Custom-House', this adventure is dismissed as 'my fellowship of toil and impracticable schemes with the dreamy bretheren of Brook Farm'. As he writes *The Scarlet Letter*, it seems to Hawthorne that the 'aged creeping past' is not only inescapable as a determining force, it also inevitably transmits into the present the corruption Emerson, Thoreau and Whitman sought to transcend. Life, therefore, is imbrued with Original Sin which, in *The Scarlet Letter* itself, Arthur Dimmesdale and Hester Prynne, as a New World Adam and Eve, have re-enacted. In this context, the scarlet 'A' is the beginning, the first letter of life, and the beginning is always the Fall. Corruption of the human body and of the body of the state is integrally at the foundation of things:

The founders of a new colony, whatever Utopia of human virtue and happiness they might originally project, have invariably recognized it among their earliest practical necessities to allot a portion of the virgin soil as a cemetery, and another portion as the site of a prison.

(Chapter 1)

Melville has written definitively of the Hawthorne so far presented, and of the 'great power of blackness in him':

Whether Hawthorne has simply availed himself of this mystical blackness as a means to the wondrous effects he makes it produce in his lights and shades; or whether there really lurks in him, perhaps unknown to himself, a touch of Puritanic gloom, – this, I cannot altogether tell. Certain it is, however, that this great power of blackness in him derives its force from its appeals to that Calvinistic sense of Innate Depravity and Original Sin, from whose visitations, in some shape or other, no deeply thinking mind is always and wholly free.[3]

This passage is famous because of the second sentence, which affirms the Hawthorne I have presented above. The hesitations Melville expresses in the first sentence, however, have not had equal attention. They point to another Hawthorne, different from the one in the second sentence. This other Hawthorne was also James's, nearly thirty years after Melville wrote the above piece. According to James: 'Nothing is more curious and interesting than this almost exclusively *imported* character of the sense of sin in Hawthorne's mind; it seems to exist there merely for an artistic or literary purpose.'[4]

Both Melville and James raise the question as to whether or not Hawthorne's sense of sin was for real. The full significance of this doubt lies in the fact that all of the above discussion of identity, history and sin hangs together. For the Hawthorne so far presented, the sense of identity determined by history was inseparable from history's moral meaning. If this meaning, derived from Original Sin, was imported, was not the entailed personal identity of guilt and torment also imported?

We might answer 'Yes' to this question, if we reconsider Hawthorne's account in 'The Custom-House' of his relationship to his ancestors. His readiness to 'take shame upon myself for their sakes' can undoubtedly be seen as the importing of an identity for the self, along with a moral stain. Hawthorne's own uneasiness with this dubious move is indicated by his pronouncement elsewhere in 'The Custom-House' that, 'the very sentiment [for the past] is an evidence that the connection, which has become an unhealthy one, should at last be severed'. Equal to this desired severance, however, was the apprehension of the futility of any independent identity he might achieve. He was convinced the futility would exist in his forebears' unbending judgement, if not always in his own. 'No aim that I have ever cherished', he writes resignedly in 'The Custom-House', 'would they recognize as laudable.'

It can be argued that by placing himself between a forbidding past and a futile present, Hawthorne was imposing enfeebling limits on his own life, if not on life as such. As Yvor Winters puts it in his characteristically incisive piece on *The Scarlet Letter*: Hawthorne 'nowhere except in the very general notion of regeneration through repentance establishes the nature of the intelligence which might exceed the intelligence of the Puritans.'[5] This conclusion is irrefutable, and I shall return to it later in my discussion of *The Scarlet Letter* itself. At this stage, I want to consider further Hawthorne's contrivance of an identity, especially his contrivance of an identity as a writer.

He always knew that his historian-editor's stance with respect to *The Scarlet Letter* was itself an importation:

> It will be seen . . . that this Custom-House sketch has a certain propriety, of a kind always recognized in literature, as explaining how a large portion of the following pages came into my possession, and as offering proofs of the authenticity of the narrative therein contained.

Scott also knew that in writing as a historian he was exploiting an established convention. Nonetheless, there is a difference between Scott and Hawthorne in this respect. In *The Heart of Midlothian*, the former is able to use the convention to write as a thoroughgoing nineteenth-century historian. His material (very much based on actual events) exists in a stable form in the past. Scott, as historian-novelist, has an assured voice in the present, where he is like a great judge, delivering a magisterial exposition of causes and effects to his jury of readers. The assumption throughout is that judge and jury will finally unite on the truth to be reached and on the moral conclusions to be drawn.

Hawthorne, however, as 'editor' of his story, is more akin to the editor Poe of *Arthur Gordon Pym* than to the editor Scott of *The Heart of Midlothian*. In the Americans' case, the editorial pose is not an understood contrivance enabling us to arrive at the firm truth of life. Rather, the question is whether there is any truth which is not contrivance. Whenever Hawthorne affects to come clean with us, therefore (putting 'myself in my true position as editor'), he is always wearing a mask. The 'Inmost Me', as he says at the beginning of 'The Custom-House', remains inevitably and forever 'behind its veil'. Unlike Scott, Hawthorne does not believe there is a common ground of truth on which writer and reader can ultimately unite. Not even self-revelation, we learn in the first paragraph of 'The Custom-House', establishes this ground:

> Some authors . . . indulge themselves in such confidential depths of revelation as could fittingly be addressed only and exclusively to the one heart and mind of perfect sympathy; as if the printed book, thrown at large on the wide world, were certain to find out the divided segment of the writer's own nature, and complete his circle of existence by bringing him into communion with it.

As we shall see, the 'circle of existence' is never completed for either author or characters in *The Scarlet Letter*. The bleak fate they share with other figures in the American scene is that subjectivity never finds a fulfilling objectivity.

The resulting covertness and instability of the authorial self are matched by the elusiveness and mutability of the past which is to be recovered. In this respect, the relationship between present and past is revealed to be always dynamic. With a volatility unsuspected by the author of *The Heart of Midlothian*, the present is believed to cause the past, as much as the past causes the present. The past, therefore, is always a variable quantity. As one changes in the present, any aspect of the past may, in Hawthorne's words towards the end of 'The Custom-House', cease 'to be a reality of my life'.

Reading such a phrase one appreciates how much Hawthorne, in the writing of fiction, is leaping forward from Scott and the stability of experience, over much of the English Victorian novel, and on towards James, Hardy, Proust and the early twentieth century. As James was to put it when asking himself about experience in 'The Art of Fiction' (1884): 'What kind of experience is intended and where does it begin and end? Experience is never limited and it is never complete.' In Hardy's words in the 1892 Preface to *Tess of the D'Urbervilles* (an altogether more developed version of some of *The Scarlet Letter*'s concerns), 'A novel is an impression not an argument.' Tess, therefore, will be seen in 'Phases' of her experience from 'Phases' of the other characters' and our experience. She will not be fixed in an argument of cause and effect, which assumes past and present are separable and identifiable quantities in unchanging causal and moral relationship.

It is in this context of the relativity of experience that we need to consider the issue of Hawthorne and the Romance. In the well-known first paragraph of the Preface to *The House of the Seven Gables* (1851), he redeployed a distinction Scott had made between the Romance and the Novel. According to Scott, the Romance was 'a fictitious narrative in prose or verse; the interest of which turns upon marvellous and uncommon incidents'. The Novel by contrast was 'a fictitious narrative, differing from the Romance, because the events are accommodated to the ordinary train of human events, and the modern state of society'.[6] In drawing on this distinction, Hawthorne was first of all making a plea that his own work should not be pressed too hard by the demands of realism. As the Preface to *The House of the Seven Gables* puts it, he wanted some space to present 'the truth of the human heart . . . under circumstances to a great extent of the writer's own choosing or creation'.

It is clear from the later Preface to *The Blithedale Romance* (1852) that Hawthorne, like Cooper before him,[7] felt the American writer to be especially disadvantaged:

In the old countries, with which fiction has long been conversant, a certain conventional privilege seems to be awarded to the romancer; his work is not put exactly side by side with nature; and he is allowed a license with regard to every day probability, in view of the improved effects which he is bound to produce thereby. Among ourselves, on the contrary, there is as yet no such Faery Land, so like the real world, that, in a suitable remoteness, one cannot well tell the difference, but with an atmosphere of strange enchantment, beheld through which the inhabitants have a propriety of their own.

Here, Hawthorne is discussing the problem also to be raised by James in his book, *Hawthorne*. I am thinking of the list of things 'absent from the texture of American life' which James provocatively drew up in Chapter 2 of that book, for example:

. . . no palaces, no castles, nor manors, nor old country-houses, nor parsonages, nor thatched cottages nor ivied ruins; no cathedrals, nor abbeys, nor little Norman churches; no great Universities nor public schools.

These items are, in Hawthorne's (for us rather weak) term, 'Faery Lands', in that they belong as much to the imagination as to reality. Any writer using such 'real' material is paradoxically already in the world of imagination. The writer in nineteenth-century America, in what James with relished exaggeration called 'this terrible denudation', is not so accommodated. Everything has to be done from a beginning which may consist of nothing but unreliable words. Everything is Romance because there is so little which passes for objective reality.

In his essay of 1824 Scott himself had affirmed what his first novel, *Waverley* (1814), had demonstrated: that some prose fictions may be both Novels and Romances. There is not in his work, however, the unavailability of objective reality we find in Hawthorne's. For Hawthorne, Romance in its most significant sense is the essential way of saying and seeing. As 'The Custom-House' puts it, it is 'moonlight, in a familiar room, . . . so unlike a morning or noontide visibility'. There is no stable, objective reality to be recovered and recorded by the stable and objective historian-novelist. There are instead creations of different lights, different points of view, different words. Among these creations are the writer's selves.

By now we have the antithesis of the Hawthorne we began with. The Hawthorne on that side of the coin is not the Hawthorne on this. As I shall show, *The Scarlet Letter* itself is always the expression of its author's double nature, or, in Lawrence's more provocative word, of its author's 'duplicity'.[8] To use Hardy's terminology, there is *The Scarlet Letter* as reassuring 'argument', especially moral argument. In this sense of the novel, life has meaning. Humanity, as represented by the allegorising Puritans, knows where it is in the developing scheme of things. But there is also *The Scarlet Letter* as seductive, unnerving 'impression'. In *this* sense of the novel, meanings elusively, endlessly change. Life is not allegory, expressing an absolute truth. It is irresolvable symbol. This latter conclusion was indeed feared not only by Hawthorne, but also by his idealistic contemporaries. For Emerson too, experience freed from the history of cause and effect might also be experience without ultimate meaning, without God. It might leave one, in Emerson's words from Chapter 7 of *Nature*, 'in the splendid labyrinth of my perceptions to wander without end'. Such was to be the fate of Miles Coverdale, Hawthorne's later authorial surrogate in *The Blithedale Romance*.

II

Hawthorne's double nature is strikingly revealed in Chapter 2, when Hester is on the scaffold with her baby:

> Had there been a Papist among the crowd of Puritans, he might have seen in this beautiful woman, so picturesque in her attire and mien, and with the infant at her bosom, an object to remind him of the image of Divine Maternity, which so many illustrious painters have vied with one another to represent; something which should remind him, indeed, but only by contrast, of that sacred image of sinless motherhood, whose infant was to redeem the world. Here, there was the taint of deepest sin in the most sacred quality of human life, working such effect, that the world was only the darker for this woman's beauty, and the more lost for the infant that she had borne.

How free from moral argument ought the imagination to range? How separable from reality, which is always defined within a moral argument, are word and image? These are the questions Hawthorne is exploring. They are complicated in the above passage by the fact that, even within a given system of reality and transcendant knowledge (in this case, Christianity), the impressions of a Puritan and a Papist might differ. For the latter, the imagination might be so ascendant that, even though this 'beautiful woman' is an adulteress, he could see in her an 'image of Divine Maternity'. There is a suggestion here that what we need to experience most profoundly, in this instance the Divine, we may only experience aesthetically through things transfigured. Nor is it one absolute image which is the source of such aesthetic experience. Images and our need of them change forever as, for example, 'so many illustrious painters' *vie* 'with one another'.

Hawthorne, in any case, will not give the imagination unreserved endorsement. He is far from asserting with Keats in 'Ode to a Grecian Urn' (1819): 'Beauty is truth, truth beauty'. Imagination may challenge moral argument. This 'beautiful woman' may transcend the label, adulteress, which the seventeenth-century community insist she wears, but 'only by contrast'. With this phrase, moral argument contests again the ground it seemed to have conceded.

For Hawthorne, as for Conrad's Marlowe in Chapter 3 of *Heart of Darkness* (1902), moral argument has to do with whether or not we finally have something to say, a position to hold. He raises this issue in the paragraph immediately following the one quoted above:

The scene was not without a mixture of awe, such as must always invest the spectacle of guilt and shame in a fellow-creature, before society shall have grown corrupt enough to smile, instead of shuddering at it. The witnesses of Hester Prynne's disgrace had not yet passed beyond their simplicity. They were stern enough to look upon her death, had that been the sentence, without a murmur at its severity, but had none of the heartlessness of another social state, which would find only a theme for jest in an exhibition like the present.

The degree of Hawthorne's support for the Puritans is very evident here. A society grown 'corrupt enough to smile' is a society with nothing to say, no positions to maintain. 'Simplicity' in this context becomes an ironic term, especially when set against 'heartlessness'. Is not the simplicity of having a moral position to be preferred to the heartlessness of having none?

If only the alternatives were so clear cut! From another point of view, the inadequacy of the Puritan position is its simplicity. It is untroubled by the doubts Hawthorne raises. The son of its god *'was* to redeem the world' (my emphasis), but all the evidence points to the failure of this mission. Because the world remains unredeemed, it is a Babel of vying images and words, without access to an absolute 'Word'. Pressed by the occasion, Hawthorne intermittently pretends to have such access. Unnerved by his imagining of Hester, he will adopt the magisterial stance of a Scott and declare the world 'only the darker for this woman's beauty, and the more lost for the infant she had borne.' Later, however, in a less threatening context, this moral argument loses its force. We are told that Pearl has sprung 'by the inscrutable decree of Providence, a lovely and immortal flower, out of the rank luxuriance of a guilty passion' (Chapter 6).

This shifting of his ground with reference to Pearl, together with the paragraphs previously quoted, is typical of the problems Hawthorne faces in establishing his bearings in *The Scarlet Letter*. As Feidelson puts it in his very important book, 'Hawthorne's subject matter is not only the meaning of adultery but also meaning in general.'[9] What seemed irrefutable terms of reference are all too likely to become no longer realities of life. 'Make way, in the King's name' (Chapter 2), cries the Beadle as he leads Hester from the prison. For Hawthorne and his readers, however, royal authority in America has been overthrown by revolution. America in 1850 has a meaning different from its meaning 'not less than two centuries ago' (Chapter 2) when the story is set. Vital institutions then, such as the scaffold, are now 'merely historical and traditional among us' (Chapter 2).

Even as Hawthorne is writing, the validity of his terms becomes questionable, so that we are continually having to negotiate with the text. This process is Romance at its most significant level, when neither author nor reader can be confident of the stability of language. At the end of Chapter 5, for example, after an account of Hester's struggle to maintain her moral sense, Hawthorne suddenly presents us with this invocation:

> O Fiend, whose talisman was that fatal symbol, woudst thou leave nothing, whether in youth or age, for this poor sinner to revere? – Such loss of faith is ever one of the saddest results of sin. Be it accepted as a proof that all was not corrupt in this poor victim of her own frailty, and man's hard law, that Hester Prynne yet struggled to believe that no fellow-mortal was guilty like herself.
>
> The vulgar, who, in those dreary old times, were always contributing a grotesque horror to what interested their imaginations, had a story about the scarlet letter which we might readily work up into a terrific legend. They averred that the symbol was

not mere scarlet cloth, tinged in an earthly dye-pot, but was red-hot with internal fire, and could be seen glowing all alight whenever Hester Prynne walked abroad in the night-time. And we must needs say it seared Hester's bosom so deeply, that perhaps there was more truth in the rumour than our modern incredulity may be inclined to admit.

One of the things to be noticed in this quotation is how unsettled Hawthorne's perspective habitually is. Although he is looking back, the past, as in the last statement of the first sentence ('such loss of faith . . .'), has such continuity with the present, one wonders what separate identity, as past, it has. This question seems to be answered by the phrase, 'those dreary old times', at the beginning of the second paragraph. This phrase has to do with the 'story about the scarlet letter'. Contrasting with it is the expression, 'our modern incredulity', at the end of the passage.

This last expression seems to distinguish the mood of time-present from the mood of time-past. If this is the case, however, it is not clear how 'our modern incredulity' is supposed to cope with the exclamation, 'O Fiend'. This invocation is certainly delivered as if it is to be accepted by Hawthorne's contemporary audience. In fact is not the whole of *The Scarlet Letter* written on the supposition that the modern audience, for all its 'incredulity' is as ready as ever the seventeenth-century Bostonians were for 'a terrific legend'? The word, 'vulgar', therefore, at the beginning of the second paragraph, is a tease. Momentarily, it lets us feel we are superior in 'our modern incredulity' to the 'vulgar' in 'those dreary old times'. In so far as we have reached Chapter 5 of 'the terrific legend' Hawthorne is working up in *The Scarlet Letter* as a whole, however, we may not be; or the allegedly 'vulgar' may not be vulgar.

I suspect Hawthorne deliberately borrowed the phrase, 'modern incredulity', from Scott's 'Life of Anne Radcliffe' (1824). In this essay Scott debates how contemporary writers of Romance can gain credence for their mysterious effects in an age when 'ancient faith' and 'modern incredulity'[10] are at odds. By showing these notions are not at odds *The Scarlet Letter* challenges Scott, but also leaves Hawthorne in a world of uncertainty as to the meaning of words. This uncertainty is conferred on his characters. In Hester's case, it arises when, of the rest of society, she begins to suspect:

. . . that the outward guise of purity was but a lie, and that, if

truth were everywhere to be shown, a scarlet letter would blaze
forth on many a bosom besides Hester Prynne's?. . . Again,
mystic sisterhood would contumaciously assert itself, as she met
the sanctified frown of some matron, who, according to the
rumour of all tongues, had kept cold snow within her bosom
throughout life. That unsunned snow in the matron's bosom,
and the burning shame on Hester Prynne's – what had the two
in common?

(Chapter 5)

What Hester expects to see in the rest of the world is the firm
morality she has transgressed. Her own identity and the world's
would then be confirmed. She is 'terror-stricken' (Chapter 5) when
this security is lost. Contraries ('unsunned snow' and 'burning
shame') 'contumaciously assert' their 'sisterhood', when Hester
wants to keep them apart. She wants certainty of meaning, even
the certainty of her identity as sinner. No more than Young
Goodman Brown, whose experience in Hawthorne's earlier story
Hester's now recalls, can Hester easily accept that 'sin is but a
name', signifying nothing. To have a certainty of self, she needs
the moral world of the Puritans and its language to be not a 'lie',
but absolute truth.

For a considerable time Hester apparently finds security in her
public identity. In Chillingworth's and Dimmesdale's cases, however, public identity is always a mask for a concealed self. The first
of these is the least developed of the three main adult characters.
He is conceived by Hawthorne less for himself than for his function with respect to Hester and Dimmesdale. He is the embodiment of knowledge as power over nature, becoming knowledge as
perverter of nature. His characterisation is also a study of the
prying observer who becomes the manipulator of another's life. In
so far as these functions inhere in the business of being a writer,
Chillingworth is a self-study for Hawthorne, as Iago is a much
greater self-study for Shakespeare. As Iago over Othello, so Chillingworth over Dimmesdale has the power of the artist unrestrained by moral argument. He becomes 'not a spectator only, but
a chief actor in the poor minister's interior world' (Chapter 11).
Significantly, the outcome of such uncurbed egotism, such vener-
ation for the conscious, knowing self, is a self-perversion (given
crude physical expression in Chillingworth's deformity) in which
Chillingworth is 'more wretched than his victim' (Chapter 11).

Although his whole life has been committed to the achievement of an ascendancy of knowledge, he finally arrives at fatalism. He tells Hester 'it has all been a dark necessity. . . . It is our fate' (Chapter 14). Perhaps this statement, with its Calvinistic overtones, is the end of egotism and the beginning of humility. Equally, it may be, as fatalism often is, the confirmation of egotism.

Dimmesdale's case is summed up by the passage at the end of Chapter 11:

It is the unspeakable misery of a life so false as his, that it steals the pith and substance out of whatever realities there are around us, and which were meant by Heaven to be the spirit's joy and nutriment. To the untrue man, the whole universe is false – it is impalpable – it shrinks to nothing within his grasp. And he himself, in so far as he shows himself in a false light, becomes a shadow, or, indeed, ceases to exist. The only truth that continued to give Mr Dimmesdale a real existence on this earth was the anguish in his inmost soul, and the undissembled expression of it in his aspect. Had he once found power to smile, and wear a face of gaiety, there would have been no such man.

In this passage time-past is again very immediate to Hawthorne. As the fabricator of authorial identities, he feels very intimate with the problem of 'the untrue man'. But how does one become the true man? To answer that this truth is achieved by complete self-revelation is to invite the response that Dimmesdale himself is said to have made in defence of Hester on the scaffold: 'that it were wronging the very nature of woman to force her to lay open her heart's secrets in such broad daylight, and in presence of so great a multitude' (Chapter 3). Such privacy, offered to every individual, would surely have the support of an author so determined to 'keep the inmost Me behind its veil'.

The problem of identity, as Hawthorne explores it, is that we need it to be both private and public. While we must have an amount of public endorsement of our sense of self, it is nonetheless vital to our freedom, even to our humanity, that our sense of self should also to an extent remain autonomous. This is why Bartleby, in Melville's story, must retain the fundamental right not to live on the world's terms, even if he can only express that right as a minimal, negative preference. In the American scene indeed it is never easy to get the private and public selves into accord. In

Dimmesdale's case, they are manifestly out of accord. Envying the label that reveals Hester to the world, he too desires, but also fears, exposure. His resulting false position means that the 'very truth' from his mouth is 'transformed . . . into the veriest falsehood' (Chapter 11). Even his true defence of Hester's right to privacy can seem, and perhaps is, a falsehood deriving from his own need for self-protection.

Becoming true, however, is not entirely in his, or any individual's, own hands. In *The Scarlet Letter*, the public world is as incapable of perceiving the individual's truth as the individual is of conveying it. To his congregation, the false Dimmesdale is 'a miracle of holiness' (Chapter 11). Even at the last, when he stands on the scaffold with Hester, he is so misunderstood that the moral Hawthorne chooses to draw ('Be true! Be true! Be true!' (Chapter 24)) is almost too blatantly ironic. 'Like *The Heart of Midlothian*', writes George Dekker, '*The Scarlet Letter* is very centrally concerned with what it means to be "true".'[11] Hawthorne's novel, however, is very unlike Scott's with regard to this issue. Hawthorne has none of Scott's certainty. For Dimmesdale being true, or attempting to be, led ultimately to his being dead. When there is no inmost me behind its veil, that moment is death. Then, we can neither agree, nor disagree, with our assigned public identities. In life, by contrast, 'the only truth that continued to give Mr Dimmesdale a real existence was the anguish in his inmost soul.' Paradoxically, this 'real existence' was occasioned by his falseness.

'To the untrue man, the whole universe is false', claims Hawthorne. The assertion, however, does not mean that Hawthorne, any more than Melville in *Moby-Dick*, believes the universe to be capable of truth. The chapter, 'The Minister's Vigil', would alone give the lie to any such proposition. This wonderfully visual and filmic chapter is, in Joycean terms, the 'Nighttown' of *The Scarlet Letter*. In standing Dimmesdale, Hester and Pearl together on the scaffold in the night, it presents the negative of the Puritans' daytime view of things. It exposes the limitations of the Puritans' (and perhaps our own) sense of normality and of a true universe, so much of which belongs only to coincident daylight. Suddenly, a strange, new light, 'doubtless caused by one of those meteors . . . burning out to waste, in the vacant regions of the atmosphere', illuminates the scene. Everything is visible,

. . . but with a singularity of aspect that seemed to give another moral interpretation to the things of this world than they had ever borne before. And there stood the minister, with his hand over his heart; and Hester Prynne, with the embroidered letter glimmering on her bosom; and little Pearl, herself a symbol, and the connecting link between those two. They stood in the noon of that strange and solemn splendour, as if it were the light that is to reveal all secrets, and the daybreak that shall unite all who belong to one another.

What purpose has the universe at this moment? What is its truth? 'None' is the answer to both these questions. Purpose cannot be claimed for the meteor, even if it is accepted as the cause of the transfiguring light. Nor does this particular light convey any more of the truth than do all the other transfiguring lights of our existence. 'As if it were *the* light' (my emphasis), it makes us aware of our need for revelation and unity without answering our need.

The rest of the chapter reveals the light to be incomprehensible in itself, even though humankind will always attempt comprehension of such manifestations. Our sense of our own stature compels us to attempt to read the universe truly, and even to assume a relationship between our own lives and the nature of the universe. We are told later in the chapter that the Puritans, in their representative way, were in the habit of trying to interpret unusual 'natural phenomena'. In Hawthorne's words, 'it was, indeed, a majestic idea, that the destiny of nations should be revealed, in these aweful hieroglyphics, on the cope of heaven.' Without such an idea, Hawthorne suggests, we are the poorer. Even so, the idea has its risks of delusion, at least in the individual case. Dimmesdale believes the light reveals to him a letter 'A' in the sky. Hawthorne concludes:

In such a case, it could only be a symptom of a highly disordered mental state, when a man, rendered morbidly self-contemplative by long, intense, and secret pain, had extended his egotism over the whole expanse of nature, until the firmament itself should appear no more than a fitting page for his soul's history and fate.

When can either the individual or the nation ever know that a reading of the universe is not egotism? Because this question is unanswerable in *The Scarlet Letter*, as it is in *Moby-Dick*, the untruth of humankind and the falseness of the universe are endless.

Dimmesdale, like Joseph K in *The Trial*, will never be able to solve his case. Nor is it the only case going on. Others are claiming attention at the same time. During this very night Governor Winthrop has died. No moment is ever uniquely one's own.

III

Hester's shock over Dimmesdale's condition in 'The Minister's Vigil' moves *The Scarlet Letter* towards its climax. In 'Another View of Hester', a chapter with a title underlining the instability of 'views', we learn that even for the Puritans the scarlet letter after seven years has taken on new meanings. We learn too that, during this time, the public identity given to Hester by the scarlet letter has become her mask for secret, personal rebellion. In a statement which must also have more recent revolutions in America and Europe in mind, Hawthorne tells us that Hester was living in an age when 'men of the sword had overthrown nobles and kings'. Hester has 'imbibed this spirit', her thoughts being so fundamental as to cause her to question, whether for 'the whole race of womanhood' 'existence [was] worth accepting even to the happiest among them'. As Hawthorne sees it, the issue is whether the identity of women can be separated, even redeemed, from their social identity, and especially from their identity as apparently entailed by men. His conclusion to a mainly sympathetic treatment of this issue is that 'a woman never overcomes these problems by any exercise of thought. They are not to be solved, or only in one way. If her heart chance to come uppermost, they vanish.'

One wonders how far the complacency of this conclusion is qualified by the words 'if' and 'chance'. As for Hawthorne's faith in a woman's 'heart', how could an author who has written 'The Interior of a Heart' chapter ever believe the heart to be an absolute, resolving force? Elsewhere, moreover, Hawthorne has given support to Hester's case as a woman by showing how much seventeenth-century New England was governed by men. 'Is there no virtue in women, save what springs from a wholesome fear of the gallows?' (Chapter 2) asks a man as the crowd waits for Hester to emerge from the gaol. Then, as now, women were expected to be a special embodiment of virtue, even as they were suspected of being virtue's most ready betrayer. Not surprisingly, those publicly estranged from this society are all women: Anne Hutchinson,

Hester Prynne, Mistress Hibbins and Pearl. In the first scene on the scaffold, the most fundamental violation of the image of madonna and child is the fact that the baby is a girl, and thus a subversion of the male centredness of the typical image. Also, by resisting the harmony of female and male which the madonna and child often depicts, Hawthorne provides a further illustration of his general belief in the broken circle of our existence. In his madonna and child, neither female nor male finds its completion in the other.

All this being said, it remains the case that Hawthorne is anxious to settle a judgement on Hester. She is, after all, always more of a challenge than the enfeebled Dimmesdale, with whom Hawthorne will indulge himself and the reader in irresolvable ironies. On the breast of Hester's gown, 'appeared the letter A. It was artistically done, and with so much fertility and gorgeous luxuriance of fancy' (Chapter 2). She is the representative of radical artistic and sexual energies, which must always assert their autonomy, and which, for good or ill, are a fundamental guarantee of our freedom. In the forest, she insists to Dimmesdale: 'What we did had a consecration of its own. We felt it so! We said so to each other' (Chapter 17). This conviction leads straight to her later, imperious appeal: 'Exchange this false life of thine for a true one. . . . Preach! Write! Act! Do anything, save to lie down and die!'

Hester expresses in the forest a passionate self-belief without which individuals may be no more than a function of the society they inhabit. Significantly, this is a rare moment in the novel in that it is released from Hawthorne's mediating exposition. One feels he wants to give these words with their fullest dramatic energy, because Hester's stance against an oppressive society and stultifying morality is one to which every individual in her position has a right. At this moment, moreover, Hester is as the voice of Emerson in, say, 'Self-Reliance' (1841). She is a version of the self in mid-nineteenth-century America, asserting its absoluteness and its freedom from the past, demanding its opportunity to begin life anew.

From this passion, however, Hawthorne immediately retreats into a voice of distanced, magisterial judgement:

Hester Prynne, with a mind of native courage and activity, and for so long a period not merely estranged but outlawed from society, had habituated herself to such latitude of speculation as was altogether foreign to the clergyman . . . Her intellect and her heart had their home, as it were, in desert places, where she roamed as freely as the wild Indian in his woods. For years past she had looked from this estranged point of view at human institutions, and whatever priests or legislators had established; criticizing all with hardly more reverence than the Indian would feel for the clerical band, the judicial robe, the pillory, the gallows, the fireside, or the church. The tendency of her fate and fortunes had been to set her free. The scarlet letter was her passport into regions where other women dared not tread. Shame, Despair, Solitude! These had been her teachers – stern and wild ones – they had made her strong, but taught her much amiss.

(Chapter 18)

Who from white civilisation, Hawthorne might go on to argue, can live in 'the wild, free atmosphere of an unredeemed, unchristian-ised, lawless region' (Chapter 18) in which Hester's passion is released? If he were reflecting on nineteenth-century American literature, he could answer: not Ishmael Bush, not Arthur Gordon Pym, not Captain Ahab, not the desolate bird in 'Out of the Cradle Endlessly Rocking', not even Natty Bumppo, who must always see this region as christianised. Dimmesdale is certainly not the man for such a venture. Furthermore, to regard lives as exchangeable is for him (and surely for Hawthorne) to regard them as meaningless. The futility of what must be forgotten would confirm the futility of was to be created. Like Hester earlier, Dimmesdale always needs the upholding structures of society, even if his position remains a false one. Once he has re-engaged with these structures during 'The New England Holiday', his commitment in the forest to Hester drains away, as she herself perceives when she witnesses him in the procession.

These general and particular arguments against Hester's stance in the forest are sound as far as they go, but they do not go far enough. Disbelief in the Emersonian faith in the absoluteness of the self, for example, need not condemn individuals to perpetual unfulfilment. It may be that in seventeenth-century New England Hester and Dimmesdale had no possibility of finding a new life. This probable historical truth, pertaining to a particular period of time, should not be presented as a universal truth. There is every sign, however, that Hawthorne is so presenting it. In the long quotation above he speaks as a generalising historian, referring to Hester's experience as a text for comment on life as such. Abstractions provide a security from which the actuality of Hester's and Dimmesdale's situation need not be considered. Magisterially summoning 'Shame, Despair, Solitude!', Hawthorne forgets that Hester's life has already been wasted by equally magisterial judgements from the Puritans.

IV

'Is this not better . . . than what we dreamed of in the forest?' (Chapter 23) asks Dimmesdale, when he is finally on the scaffold in public. Hester is unpersuaded, and the minister's question may imply some doubt on his part. He has just delivered the 'Election Sermon'. According to the testimony of his hearers:

> Never had a man spoken in so wise, so high, and so holy a spirit, as he that spake this day; nor had inspiration ever breathed through mortal lips more evidently than it did through his.
> (Chapter 23)

Were these words sincere on Dimmesdale's part, or were they performance? It may be that even at this stage Hawthorne is maintaining the irresolvability of this question. Perhaps his own judgement of Hester in the quotation above was performance. Sincerely or insincerely, however, one can always choose which performance to give.

Dimmesdale's final self-glorification certainly is at Hester's expense, in that it entails her acceptance of life-long penance as an adulteress. All along, it seems that Hester for both Dimmesdale and Hawthorne has been one more of the 'male-engendered female figures [who] have incarnated man's ambivalence not only toward female sexuality but toward [his] own (male) physicality.'[12] Even as we accuse the dying Dimmesdale of presumption, however, we should go in the opposite direction and recognise his ultimate attempt, at his last opportunity for pronouncement, *not* to presume. I am thinking of his affirmation that 'God shall order' (Chapter 23). Unless this affirmation is the greatest presumption! For Pearl, this last scene on the scaffold repairs the family structure, the brokenness of which Hawthorne has required her, too insistently and too repetitively, to express. Now, 'she would grow up amid human joy and sorrow, nor forever do battle with the world, but be a woman in it' (Chapter 13). How typically provocative even the conclusive tone of this statement is! 'Be a woman'! Is it not a contention of *The Scarlet Letter* that we do not know what these three words mean, any more than we know what the two words, 'Be true', mean? In fact, we do not know for sure what happens to Pearl.

Despite the author's argument, therefore, the novel's ending is as inconclusive as its beginning may be unbelievable. *When* was its beginning? Was it in the forest outside Boston, in the Old World where Hester and Chillingworth were married, or in the Garden of Eden where Adam and Eve committed the Original Sin? 'No story of love was surely ever less of a "love story"', concluded James,[13] in a judgement that cuts more ways than one. In one sense, it is appropriate that the beginning ('the story of love') should be an incredible affair. The human situation is always inherited, its alleged beginnings always in a world elsewhere, unreachable from the world we inhabit. In another sense, however, James's pronouncement supports the suspicion that all Hawthorne's ambiguities and ironies are at the expense of the passion and energy, which would have been at the heart of a 'real' relationship, and which for good or ill would have had their way. Had they been present, we might, for example, have had something other than the triviality of 'The Minister in a Maze'. Should we be forgetting, this chapter alone reminds us that *The Scarlet Letter*, in its treatment of the individual's sense of self in a morally ambiguous universe, is not anything of the stature of *Macbeth*, *The Brothers Karamazov*, or *Moby-Dick*.

4

Melville: *Moby-Dick* (1851)

In no other work of American literature do the fundamental American questions, about the nature of the self and the world and about the relationship between the self and the world, have the heroic scale and tragic development they have in *Moby-Dick*. Nor does any other American work, in exploring these questions, submit literary form to such strain. I shall begin my demonstration of these claims by discussing two well-known episodes in the book. They are from 'The Mast-Head' and 'The Quarter-Deck', two chapters placed one after the other.

In the first of these chapters, we immediately meet the narrator in characteristic voice. It reminds us of the Defoe of *Robinson Crusoe* (1719), crossed with the Sterne of *Tristram Shandy* (1760) and the Carlyle of *Sartor Resartus* (1836). Defoe is there in the documentation of facts about standing on mastheads, Sterne and Carlyle in the exhortation and exclamation, and in the humorous analogies to standing on mastheads, ranging from the ancient Egyptians ascending their pyramids, to Nelson on top of his column. As often in *Moby-Dick*, it is exhilarating to be reading a writer who has had momentous adventures away from the desk. Such experience frequently enables Melville to sustain with a vivid actuality his reflections on the nature of life. Typically, the exposition of facts about whaling is transformed into a context for enacting and debating a metaphysical or philosophical problem. In 'The Mast-Head', we eventually arrive at the following account of what might happen to one of the 'many romantic, melancholy, and absent-minded young men' who finds himself perched aloft:

> . . . lulled into such an opium-like listlessness of vacant unconscious reverie is this absent-minded youth by the blending cadence of waves with thoughts, that at last he loses his identity; takes the mystic ocean at his feet for the visible image of that deep, blue, bottomless soul, pervading mankind and nature;

and every strange, half-seen, gliding, beautiful thing that eludes him; every dimly-discovered, uprising fin of some indiscernible form, seems to him the embodiment of those elusive thoughts that only people the soul by continually flitting through it. In this enchanted mood, thy spirit ebbs away to whence it came; becomes diffused through time and space; like Cranmer's sprinkled Pantheistic ashes, forming at last a part of every shore the round globe over.

There is no life in thee, now, except that rocking life imparted by a gently rolling ship; by her, borrowed from the sea, by the sea, from the inscrutable tides of God. But while this sleep, this dream is on ye, move your foot or hand an inch; slip your hold at all; and your identity comes back in horror. Over Descartian vortices you hover. And perhaps, at mid-day, in the fairest weather, with one half-throttled shriek you drop through that transparent air into the summer sea, no more to rise for ever. Heed it well, ye Pantheists![1]

According to Emerson in 'The American Scholar' (1837), 'nature is the opposite of the soul, answering to it part for part'. Most of this passage is an enactment of that proposition. In it there is an essential harmony between the soul of the individual and the soul of nature or the world. Burdens of individual identity are lost in 'that deep, blue, bottomless soul, pervading mankind and nature'. All becomes one; one becomes all.

Similar moments of Transcendental communion, achieving a resolution of what I have called the fundamental American questions, can be found in Emerson (the 'transparent eyeball' passage in Chapter 1 of *Nature* (1836)), in Thoreau ('The Bean-Field' chapter of *Walden* (1850)), in Whitman (poem 5 of 'Song of Myself'). Of all these examples, Melville's realisation of Transcendental experience is the most convincing. In the first sentence of the second paragraph above he gives this experience a wonderful actuality. Standing thus on the masthead, swaying to 'the inscrutable tides of God', one might indeed feel in communion with energies beyond the self, but also sustaining the self and the world.

It is typical of nineteenth-century American literature that while such an experience as this might be vividly evoked, it nonetheless retains an abstract and polarised quality. There is the self and nature, the self and the world, the self and God, but nothing, except the possibility of Transcendental communion, in between: no accommodating customs, ceremonies or history; no familiarising human attributes to divinity. To descend from the heightened moment, therefore, is always to return to the unaccommodated self. In this instance, in Melville's unforgettable comment on the nature of the self, 'your identity comes back in horror'. Only humour remains as a relieving resource. Melville is thoroughly American[2] in a way he uses humour as an end in itself to fill his gaps, in this instance between the actual and the transcendent. At the beginning of the passage, humour had enabled Melville to establish some distance on the 'absent-minded young man'. It seems to give him a wiser perspective the young man does not have. As the passage proceeds, however, the imagined youth and the authorial voice become as one and are only minimally reseparated in the final, desperately jocular injunction: 'Heed it well, ye Pantheists!'

I am writing of the author, Melville, and not of the narrator, Ishmael, because at this stage in *Moby-Dick* Ishmael has obviously disappeared. Once the voyage begins, Ishmael has only an intermittent and insubstantial presence, either as narrator or character. His invisibility points to *Moby-Dick*'s major formal problem, which is Melville's inability to establish a perspective on the book's experience. I shall return to this formal problem and to Ishmael later. At this stage I want to draw attention to the related issue of Melville's presence in *Moby-Dick*, and to argue that as he writes the book he exists nowhere but in the book. As is the case with much nineteenth-century American literature, we have little sense in *Moby-Dick* of an attendant, objective world in which author, reader and the book might find a sustaining life. Just as the voyage of the *Pequod* is an attempt to discover and identify an American self and its New World, so the writing of *Moby-Dick* is an attempt to discover and identify an American authorial self and its New World. In each case the search is for subject and object, and a relationship between subject and object.

The inspiring energy of the voyage is Ahab. In contrast to the figure on the masthead, he no longer gets the heightened moment, if he ever had it. His identity is unrelieved horror, projected onto, or projected from, the external world, represented for him by Moby Dick: 'the White Whale swam before him as the monomaniac incarnation of all those malicious agencies which some

deep men feel eating in them' (Chapter 41). The heart of the matter
as far as Ahab is concerned is expressed in his speech to Starbuck
in 'The Quarter-Deck':

> All visible objects, man, are but as pasteboard masks.[3] But in
> each event – in the living act, the undoubted deed – there, some
> unknown but still reasoning thing puts forth the moulding of its
> features from behind the unreasoning mask. If man will strike,
> strike through the mask! How can the prisoner reach outside
> except by thrusting through the wall? To me, the white whale is
> that wall, shoved near to me. Sometimes I think there's naught
> beyond. But 'tis enough. He tasks me; he heaps me; I see in him
> outrageous strength, with an inscrutable malice sinewing it.
> That inscrutable thing is chiefly what I hate; and be the white
> whale agent, or be the white whale principal, I will wreak that
> hate upon him. . . . Who's over me?

Ahab feels no connection with anything beyond the self. His very
existence, therefore, remains unconfirmed. He speaks of 'the living act' and 'the undoubted deed', because he is as oppressed as
are Hamlet and Macbeth by experience of the act which is *un*living
and the deed which is doubted. He cannot bear the irresolvable
mask of creation and its apparent indifference to the individual
life. By heroic, violent action he intends to break from what he sees
as his prison and to 'strike through the mask'. In the ensuing
grand climax, he hopes truth will be revealed: the truth that the
energies of the self are equal to, and at one with, the energies of
creation. According to Emerson in Chapter 3 of *Nature*, 'Nature
stretches out her arms to embrace man, only let his thoughts be
equal greatness.' For Ahab the whole voyage is an attempt to
achieve this kind of transcendent harmony between the self and
the world. His desperate tones, however, betray his suspicion that
such resolution will forever elude him. It may well be that no
aspect of the mask of life (be that aspect the whale or whatever)
will express anything other than itself. 'Who's over me?' demands
Ahab, not only in defiance, but also as a genuine question. He
needs to know whether his life alone is the measure of his life.

　His stance is so American in that it is so fundamental, returning
us again to the unaccommodated self. Unless this American self
can respond to its New World with an original energy equal to the

New World's, it knows, as does Whitman in the first two lines of poem 25 of 'Song of Myself', that it will face annihilation. In scenes such as the one above, Melville employs a Shakespearean dramatic mode and leans on the Shakespeare of the tragedies to find a voice for Ahab. But whereas in *King Lear*, for example, the play has to work towards 'unaccommodated man'[4] by breaking its way through a heritage of structures and expectations, with Ahab we begin in unaccommodation. It is as if the compromises of history have not happened, or have been of no avail. Adam has never been consoled: 'I feel', Ahab is to say later, 'as though I were Adam, staggering beneath the piled centuries since Paradise' (Chapter 132).

He has none of the purity of experience of Adam unfallen in the New World, such as Thoreau and Whitman can imagine for the American self. For Ahab what might have been purity is instead an appalling blankness (see 'The Whiteness of the Whale'), unfilled by and resistant to Old World consciousness. In Chapter 18 of *The Scarlet Letter* this territory is 'the wild, free atmosphere of an unredeemed, unchristianised, lawless region'. But while Hawthorne and his characters retreat from this region, Melville's and Ahab's whole endeavour is to assert the self in it and compel recognition from it. With Hamlet and Shakespeare's other tragic heroes, Ahab longs for the ultimate moment when he can say: 'My fate cries out'.[5]

Melville asks us to recognise Ahab's quest as heroic and, therefore, capable of tragedy, even as *Moby-Dick* in common with Shakespeare's plays is questioning the very terms of heroism and tragedy with reference to which we might debate the book's experience. As is the case with Hamlet, Macbeth and Lear, Ahab's quest takes him to the heart of the unanswerable, experience of which becomes an occasion for atrocity. Inevitably, we will make a moral response to enterprises of this kind and criticise the actions of the protagonist. If we are to be appropiate to *Moby-Dick*, however, we should understand that is it not merely Ahab's culpability that takes him to the point of no return. The tragedy, as realised in the voyage as a whole, is the expression of fundamental contradictions in human nature and in life itself. It is the outcome of 'probings at the very axis of reality'.

This last phrase is from 'Hawthorne and his Mosses',[6] the now famous review, written by Melville with American literature, *Moby-Dick* and Shakespearean tragedy very much on his mind:

. . . those occasional flashings-forth of the intuitive Truth in him; those short, quick probings at the very axis of reality – these are the things that make Shakespeare, Shakespeare. Through the mouths of the dark characters of Hamlet, Timon, Lear, and Iago, he craftily says, or sometimes insinuates the things, which we feel to be so terrifically true, that it were all but madness for any good man, in his own proper character, to utter or even hint of them. Tormented into desperation, Lear the frantic King tears off the mask, and speaks the sane madness of vital truth.

The mutually questioning terms ('madness', 'mask', 'truth') in which Melville is reading Shakesperian tragedy are also the mutually questioning terms in which he is imagining Ahab's quest:

All that most maddens and torments; all that stirs up the lees of things; all truth with malice in it; all that cracks the sinews and cakes the brain; all the subtle demonisms of life and thought; all evil to crazy Ahab, were visibly personified, and made practicably assailable in Moby Dick. He piled upon the whale's white hump the sum of all the general rage and hate felt by his whole race for Adam down.

(Chapter 41)

From the above passage there is no doubt that Melville himself has experienced 'all that most maddens and torments . . .'. The 'malice' Ahab sees in Moby Dick is to be supported later by Melville's own sense of the whale's 'malignity' (Chapter 41), and of the 'horrible vulturism' (Chapter 69) of life itself. As in Shakespeare's tragedies, we are not allowed to decide that the central figure has become entirely mad, even though the charge of madness is laid against him in *Moby-Dick* by the author himself.

One of the functions of the phrase 'crazy Ahab' is indeed to separate Melville from Ahab. It is as if the author suspects what the last quotation betrays: that he is being too excitedly swept along by his conception of Ahab. This point returns us to the problem of perspective or point of view. As narrator, Ishmael should have resolved this problem for Melville by helping to distance the author from the work he was creating. Allegedly, it is Ishmael who delivers the account of Ahab quoted above. At the beginning of the chapter, 'Moby Dick', from which the passage was taken, Ishmael bursts back into the book with these words:

I, Ishmael was one of the crew; my shouts had gone up with the rest; my oath had been welded with theirs; and stronger I shouted, and more did I hammer and clinch my oath, because of the dread in my soul. A wild, mystical, sympathetical feeling was in me; Ahab's quenchless feud seemed mine.

All readers will note these words, as they try to get a fix on Ishmael and on his development. It is not clear, however, how someone, who makes the declaration above, could then go on to pronounce Ahab 'crazy'. Did Ishmael believe Ahab to be 'crazy' at the very time when 'Ahab's quenchless feud seemed mine'? In any case, how does this re-emergence of fundamental alienation in Ishmael develop from his earlier redemption from this condition in Chapter 10 by Queequeg, who is also on the voyage?

These are only some of the questions raised by any attempt to see Ishmael as narrator and character, offering us a perspective on the book. *Moby-Dick* might have been the story of Ishmael's life, or of a significant period of it. It might have been a time-past told from the perspective of the end, which is time-present. In a big book, this is never a straightforward procedure, as the opening sentence of *David Copperfield* (1849–50) makes clear. Yet, in this respect, *Moby-Dick* is unsettled to an extent unimagined by Dickens.

II

'Call me Ishmael'; 'Let me call myself, for the present, William Wilson'; 'You don't know about me, without you have read a book by the name of "The Adventures of Tom Sawyer".' Ishmael is one of several nineteenth-century American narrators whose identity is being assumed only for the immediate purposes of fiction. Unlike the David of *David Copperfield*, these narrators make little if any claim to an established identity beyond their story, to which their story had contributed. There is no implication that they are narrating from a settled position at the end. The proposition is rather that they are seeking identity in worlds which are inchoate and plotless. The continuing instability of their voices is a confirmation of this proposition.

Ishmael's is never a settled voice. Consider the book's second sentence: 'Some years ago – never mind how long precisely'. In response to this statement it may seem pedantic to want to know when Ishmael's adventures took place. No one wants dates, but when, in relation to wherever he is now, did Ishmael's adventures happen? When, for example, was Ishmael like this?

> As for me, I am tormented with an everlasting itch for things remote. I love to sail forbidden seas, and land on barbarous coasts. Not ignoring what is good, I am quick to perceive a horror, and could still be social with it – would they let me – since it is well to be on friendly terms with all the inmates of the place one lodges in.
>
> (Chapter 1)

To be so restless for extreme adventure (and jocular about it) is understandable before the disaster of the *Pequod's* voyage, but not when it is over and one is supposedly reflecting on it. Yet it is impossible to decide when Ishmael was like this. Similarly, we do not know when Ishmael has the inner resource, with its Emersonian distinction between the 'Me' and the 'Not me',[7] described in the following passage:

> Methinks my body is but the lees of my better being. In fact take my body who will, take it, I say, it is not me. And therefore three cheers for Nantucket; and come a stove boat and stove body when they will, for stave my soul, Jove himself cannot.
>
> (Chapter 7)

He is to offer a variation of this sense of himself many chapters later in 'The Grand Armada';

> Even so, amid the tornadoed Atlantic of my being, do I for ever centrally disport in mute calm; and while ponderous planets of unwaning woe revolve round me, deep down and deep inland there I still bathe me in eternal mildness of joy.

How do any of these last three passages relate to the Ishmael who, before he met Queequeg, tells us of a 'splintered heart and maddened hand . . . turned against the wolfish world' (Chapter 10)? How does the Ishmael, who always has access to 'eternal mildness of joy', ever declare 'Ahab's quenchless feud seemed mine'?

Melville's comments in the first lines of the chapters 'The Crotch' and 'The Honour and Glory of Whaling' reveal his pervading consciousness of *Moby-Dick* as a difficult task to be accomplished. In this connection, 'Some years ago – never mind how long precisely' is a disarming joke to put the reader in a compliant mood. Elsewhere Melville wonders how Ahab is to be created ('The Specksynder'), and how to convince us that whales can ram ships ('The Battering-Ram'). *Moby-Dick*, however, lacks any other kind of presiding consciousness or self-awareness. The result is that readers, with everything left on their hands, may well wonder what authority they have for making any connections. Father Mapple, for example, ends his sermon with the profound question: 'What is man that he should live out the lifetime of his God?' (Chapter 9). His humility provides a reference point from which to assess Ahab's egotism and monomania, but since no one in the book remembers Mapple's words for the next six hundred pages, one wonders if one should do so oneself. Does it contribute to Queequeg's or the whale's significance that the phallus of the whale is 'jet-black as Yojo, the ebony idol of Queequeg' (Chapter 95)? Is the rescue of Tashtego by Queequeg from the head of a whale ('The Prairie') anything more than an intriguing incident, done for its own sake? Mid-way through *Moby-Dick* it can become very difficult to sustain a consciousness of whatever thematic concerns the book is supposed to have.

III

What was on Melville's hands in *Moby-Dick*, however, resisted mightily the kind of accomplishment the above comments are looking for. Ishmael sometime speaks in the same tones as Ahab, and both characters can be forgotten by Melville, because both Ishmael and Ahab are never more than voices of their creator. With Ishmael and Ahab, Melville himself is seeking a sense of an ending, a sense of confirmation, for the American self in the New World. As in the work of other writers in this book, none is found. Melville's great adventure story has a grand climax, but no end except death. *Moby-Dick* is without perspective, without a presiding consciousness, because there is no end on the way to death from which to voice perspective and consciousness. As in *Huckleberry Finn*, there is survival only in the name of survival.

Moby-Dick goes through the motions of being in a past tense, but its time, like the time of *Arthur Gordon Pym* and *Huckleberry Finn*, is always the perspectiveless present of the New World. Not surprisingly, therefore, the book is full of a sense of the irresolvable. The voyage takes place on the mirror of the sea, in which like 'Narcissus' (Chapter 1), we may see only a transformed version of ourselves, and which in itself is 'an everlasting terra incognita' (Chapter 58). Its course is 'round the world' (Chapter 52), with 'not a voyage complete' (Chapter 8). To try to understand the whale, in its 'colourless, all-colour' (Chapter 42), is to attempt 'the classification of the constituents of a chaos' (Chapter 32). The whale is marked by 'undecipherable hieroglyphics' (Chapter 68). It has 'no face' (Chapter 86), the front of its head being 'a dead blind wall, without a single organ or tender prominence of any sort whatever' (Chapter 76). A sperm-whale skeleton, worshipped by the natives in the Arsacides, is found to have 'no living thing within; naught was there but bones'. As vines weave themselves through it, it belongs only to unending organic process: 'Life folded Death; Death trellised Life' (Chapter 102).

Amid its overwhelming sense of the irresolvable, amid its sense of the unceasing multiplicity of analogies and interpretations (in, for example, 'Extracts' at the beginning and the 'gams' throughout), *Moby-Dick* nonetheless strives to believe with Ahab that 'some certain significance lurks in all things' (Chapter 99). Ahab's quest for certainty is given powerful authorial endorsement, because Melville, even with the resource of his humour, cannot easily settle for the irresolvable. *Moby-Dick* is not pointing a moral and indicating we should aim to be more like the jocular Ishmael than the monomaniacal Ahab. In so far as the two figures are distinct characterisations, each exists as a complement to, and justification of, the other. The voyage of the *Pequod*, as a representative human enterprise, is an affirmation of significance in itself and also a quest for significance. At a basic level it is how a living might be earned, though none of us would put ourselves at such risk for money alone. As exemplified in 'The First Lowering', the voyage speaks to a deeper need in us for ultimate experience, to find the measure of the self and the truth of the world. 'Be it life or death', argues Thoreau, who as a nineteenth-century American necessarily had his life and a world to settle, 'we crave only reality',[8] But whereas in Thoreau the craving is expressed deliberately and individually, paring away the superfluous to reach the essential and eventually arriving at a creatively passive receptivity, in *Moby-Dick* it is expressed in heroic communal action on the major scale: a 'deputation from all the isles of the sea, and all the ends of the earth, accompanying old Ahab in the *Pequod* to lay the world's grievances before that bar from which not very many of them ever come back' (Chapter 27).

The ominousness of these last words indicates that the voyage is not uncritically romanticised. It can indeed occasion atrocity:

> And now abating in his flurry, the whale once more rolled out into view; surging from side to side; spasmodically dilating and contracting his spout-hole, with sharp, cracking, agonized respirations. At last, gush after gush of clotted red gore, as if it had been the purple lees of red wine, shot into the frighted air; and falling back again, ran dripping down his motionless flanks into the sea. His heart had burst!
>
> 'He's dead, Mr Stubb,' said Daggoo.
>
> 'Yes; both pipes smoked out!' and withdrawing his own from his mouth, Stubb scattered the dead ashes over the water; and, for a moment, stood thoughtfully eyeing the vast corpse he had made.
>
> (Chapter 61)

Consciously or unconsciously, Stubb's response represses despair, anguish, horror, dread, madness. Any one of these responses, or others of the same order, might be ours at the realisation that our very life, our quest as in whale-hunting for the means of light itself, has led to such slaughter. Melville is one of the very few novelists writing in English who can capture the essential tragedy of the human condition, in which the great, adventurous, courageous positives of our being become also its murderous negatives. The momentousness of the violence here is vividly emphasised by the allusion (in the blood as 'red wine') to the sacrificed body of Christ. The question arises as to whether this violence exists only within humanity, or whether it is also integral to nature itself? In 'The Grand Armada', when we gaze wondrously with Melville in the depths of the sea at 'the nursing mothers of the whales, and those that by their enormous girth seemed shortly to become mothers', and at 'the young of these whales', we may tend to the first alternative. In the company of the

sharks, which 'viciously snapped, not only at each other's disem-
bowelments, but like flexible bows, bent round and bit their own'
(Chapter 66), the second alternative persuades.

Moby-Dick, therefore, is trying to realise, explore, and come to
terms with, the essential condition of our existence, not as social
beings living in developed historical contexts, but as fragments in
the elemental New World. All the characterisations and the fictional, as opposed to the documentary, situations are variations on
this theme. Melville is doing the American scene in the nineteenth
century in different voices. While there are not many of these
voices, there are enough to give us points of reference for human
response amid the immensity of the non-human which the book so
unforgettably presents.

'Stubb Kills a Whale' was one of these points of reference.
Among others, there are Father Mapple, Bulkington, Starbuck and
Pip. The first represents resignation to the incomprehensible,
awesome order of God. Not even the violent contradictions of
Mapple's own service of God ('Delight is to him, who . . . kills,
burns and destroys all sin' (Chapter 9)) shakes his faith in God and
resignation to God's will. Bulkington, as briefly treated in 'The Lee
Shore', is forever unrewarded and unaccommodated until death.
The end of one lonely voyage in search of 'the highest truth' is but
the beginning of the next. Starbuck is presented in the first of the
'Knights and Squires' chapters. Courageous and admirably normal
man that he is, it is nonetheless clear where his courage ends and
his caution begins. The characterisation is especially being used to
set off the grander conception and greater stature of Ahab. Finally,
there is Pip. From his fate in 'The Castaway', we discover that,
alone, thrust ultimately on the self, unsupported by any context of
life, we may be overwhelmed and maddened. In the middle of a
chase, Pip jumps out of Starbuck's boat and is abandoned in the
ocean: 'the intense concentration of self in the middle of such a
heartless immensity, my God! who can tell it?' This pronouncement takes us back to the 'heartless voids and immensities of the
universe' at the end of 'The Whiteness of the Whale'. To be cast
away amid such voids is the representative American fate, repeatedly imagined by the literature discussed in this book. The
literature is trying to 'tell it' and overcome it. From 'the intense
concentration of self' the writers seek fulfilling intercourse with the
reader, as Ahab seeks fulfilling intercourse with the world.

None of *Moby-Dick*'s characterisations is complicated. Each exists as an illustration of a single state of being. Even in Ahab's case, the great 'strike through the mask' speech is very nearly all there is to him. As we might expect, he goes on to express self-doubt, especially in 'The Symphony'. Such a moment of self-awareness confirms that Ahab has indeed 'his humanities' (Chapter 16). It qualifies the authoritarianism and demagoguery to which Melville knows a heroic leader may well be prone. Between the positions of wilful resolve and doubtful self-questioning, however, there are long stretches of *Moby-Dick* when Ahab is entirely unavailable to us. When he is available, we may have, as in 'The Candles', only the unreadable sound and fury of his posture.

Moby-Dick would undoubtedly be a greater book if its background 'material' were matched by a foreground human drama of equal stature. It is a matter of fact, nevertheless, that apart from a few moments in Cooper and Hawthorne (more so in the latter), there is little in the way of complicated human interinvolvement in the American novel until we get to James. There are not the supporting historical and social structures from which such interinvolvements derive. It was to have access to structures of this kind that James left America for Europe. Certainly no writer in America was suggesting ways of doing a human drama which would be equal in scale to the other forces in *Moby-Dick*.

Shakespeare, who obviously inspired Melville, was of limited use to a novelist. Melville was struggling with a form requiring an extended linear structure and characters living in a solidly specified cause and effect world. Such is not the business of what the Prologue to *Romeo and Juliet* announces as 'the two hours' traffic of our stage'. In so far as Shakespeare has contributed to the creation of Ahab, therefore, and in so far as Ahab is actually created in Shakespearian dramatic terms, so much will the character be unavailable for the kind of business and development the novel form requires. Furthermore, there is the question of what there remains for Melville to achieve with a Shakespearian Ahab, that Shakespeare himself has not already achieved with Hamlet, Macbeth, Lear, Timon and Coriolanus. Matthiessen raises this question in an alternative form, when he points out that some of Ahab's speeches seem 'never to have belonged to the speaker, to have been at best a ventriloquist's trick'.[9] So obsessed is Melville by Shakespeare, he risks being buried by him. This danger is avoided in Twain's necessary irreverence ('To be, or not to be; that is the bare bodkin' (*Huckleberry Finn*, Chapter 21)) for the bard.

Even Ishmael's and Queequeg's relationship exists for a single illustrative purpose. This purpose having been achieved, in those irresistible opening chapters, there is little more to do with Queequeg. For the most part he can be 'forgotten', in Lawrence's words, 'like yesterday's newspaper'.[10] He is in *Moby-Dick* to present with Ishmael the ideal of the relationship between the white Christian and the pagan aboriginal.[11] The ideal has its antithesis in the diabolism of Ahab and Fedallah, while the consequences of the failure of the ideal for America are remembered in the fate of the Pequod Indians, after whom Ahab's ship is named. Themselves apparently a warlike people, the Pequod Indians were exterminated in the seventeenth century by American colonists. Ishmael's and Queequeg's relationship is very different from the Crusoe/ Friday, master/servant, relationship in *Robinson Crusoe*. Indeed it bears an unexpected resemblance to Hamlet and Horatio, the troubled Ishmael projecting onto Queequeg the equanimity he himself is without: 'He seemed entirely at his ease, preserving the utmost serenity; content with his own companionship; always equal to himself.' As Ishmael and Queequeg eventually lie in bed together, 'a cosy loving pair' (Chapter 10), Ishmael is rescued from 'the step-mother world' (Chapter 132), which is to remain Ahab's, and there is a suggestion, in this nearly womanless and perhaps misogynist book, that Queequeg is the mate Adam really wanted, and, in the New World, still wants.

In the search for a relationship between the masculine self and the New World, women have been left behind on the shores of compromise and corruption, never to be returned to. Such is the deep and unresolved Adamic energy in *Moby-Dick*. Even if this energy were capable of resolution, Melville would have to go further with Ishmael and Queequeg than he dares. In a well-known reflection in the chapter 'A Squeeze of the Hand', the domestic life, of which 'the wife' is the first representative, is recognised as a tempting solace. It is something one might settle for in lowering one's 'conceit of attainable felicity', that is, in abandoning the quest. In an English *Moby-Dick*, the narrator at this point might well have conceded, transferred during a 'gam' to a boat going home, married the girl he had left behind and settled down. I think, for example, of Captain Robert Warren, the narrator of *Frankenstein* (1818), abandoning his quest in Chapter 24 to return to 'dear England and the dearer friends that inhabit it'. In Melville's American book the narrative voice remains unaccommodated to the end. 'Would that I could keep squeezing that sperm for ever!' he exclaims. Yet the communion with the men, which the episode reports and reflects on, was 'a strange sort of insanity' and, with 'the wife', would belong to a fantasy. This fantasy becomes 'visions of the night, [where] I saw long rows of angels in paradise, each with his hands in a jar of spermaceti'. Human relationships for Ishmael/Melville are always fantastical or dream-like. As on other occasions in *Moby-Dick*, the void at the heart of the whole reflection in 'A Squeeze of the Hand' is made bearable only because of the humour which informs the reflection. The humour, even so, leaves the narrator completely unplaced. He speaks of a 'now', as a point from which he has been able to assemble these particular passing thoughts. This 'now', however, is nowhere.

> And I, and Silence, some strange Race
> Wrecked, solitary, here –[12]

Dickinson's representative American nightmare in which 'Sense' breaks, leaving her 'Wrecked, solitary, here –', which is nowhere, oppressed by the only end, which is death, is also Melville's on the grander scale. It is Whitman's too, as voiced by the desolated bird in 'Out of the Cradle endlessly Rocking'. Against the 'silence' of the whale (Chapter 79), any 'sense' Melville achieves is always momentary, precarious and reversible. 'Man, in the ideal, . . . so noble and so sparkling, . . . that democratic dignity which, on all hands, radiates without end from God' (Chapter 26), becomes, as the famous chapter 'The Try-Works' vividly reveals, man hell bent.

To keep such reversals at bay where does one turn, if not to the sustaining manners of life implied by 'the wife, the heart, the bed, the table, the saddle, the fire-side, the country' (Chapter 95), or by their equivalents? Sustenance of this kind is available to the English Captain Boomer in 'Leg and Arm'. Having encountered Moby Dick and lost an arm, Boomer knows when he has had enough. He has a life to settle back on, as evidenced in his relations with his first mate, Mounttop, and his ship's surgeon, Dr Bunger (all these names are obviously suggestive). The last, in any case, assures Boomer and Ahab that 'what you take for the White Whale's malice is only his awkwardness. For he never means to swallow a single limb; he only thinks to terrify by feints.'

Neither Ishmael, nor Ahab, nor Melville can settle in this way.

Except marginally in Cooper, 'the wife, the heart, the bed, the table, the saddle, the fire-side, the country' receive no blessing in the American literature discussed in this book. The New World in this literature is not Boomer's and Bunger's. As represented by Moby Dick, it remains utterly uncontainable and unresolvable: 'not Jove, not that great majesty Supreme did surpass the glorified White Whale as he so divinely swam' (Chapter 133); but then: 'retribution, swift vengeance, eternal malice were in his whole aspect' (Chapter 135).

No other writer of prose fiction in English presents nature so awesomely as does Melville in *Moby-Dick*. Only Hardy approaches him thirty years later. Melville can be a tediously long-winded writer when he philosophises. As Lawrence says: 'He preaches and holds forth because he is not sure of himself. And he holds forth, often, so amateurishly.' But such moments as the third paragraph of 'The Whiteness of the Whale' and the last three paragraphs of 'The Try-Works' are more than compensated for, as Lawrence also saw, by chapters such as 'The Mat-Maker', 'The First Lowering', 'The Spirit-Spout', 'The *Pequod* meets the Albatross', 'Brit', 'Squid', 'Stubb Kills a Whale', 'The Shark Massacre', 'The *Pequod* Meets the *Virgin*', 'The Grand Armada' and 'The Castaway'. Reading these chapters and deliberating over *Moby-Dick*, I am often reminded of Eliot's lines at the end of 'East Coker' (1940):

> Through the dark cold and the empty desolation,
> The wave cry, the wind cry, the vast waters
> Of the petrel and the porpoise. In my end is my beginning.

The lines are wonderfully evocative. So little of what they evoke, however, has any presence in the body of the poem they conclude. So much of it has great presence in *Moby-Dick*.

5

Whitman: *Leaves of Grass*

In its American way, the 'I' of 'Song of Myself' (1855)[1] remains as unresolved and as disintegrated as the 'I' of either *Arthur Gordon Pym*, or *Moby-Dick*, or *Huckleberry Finn*. In this respect it contrasts as much with the more settled 'I' of Wordsworth's *The Prelude* (1805) as does Huck with the Pip of *Great Expectations* (1861). I make this claim despite the apparent confidence about the self pro-claimed in the opening line of 'Song of Myself' and regularly thereafter. Such moments of assurance in Whitman are always the proclamation of a thesis against which the antithesis is pressing starkly and destructively. This precariousness is evident even in the final poem of 'Song of Myself', when we might have expected the work as a whole to have reached its reassuring destination, and the 'I' to be able to 'suppose', as can the 'I' at the end of *The Prelude*, 'my powers so far confirmed':[2]

The spotted hawk swoops by and accuses me, he complains
   of my gab and my loitering.

I too am not a bit tamed, I too am untranslatable,
I sound my barbaric yawp over the roofs of the world.

The last scud of day holds back for me,
It flings my likeness after the rest and true as any
   on the shadow'd wilds,
It coaxes me to the vapour and the dusk.

I depart as air, I shake my white locks at the runaway sun,
   I effuse my flesh in eddies, and drift it in lacy jags.

I bequeathe myself to the dirt to grow from the grass I love,
   If you want me again look for me under your boot-soles.

You will hardly know who I am or what I mean,
But I shall be good health to you nevertheless,
And filter and fibre your blood.

Failing to fetch me at first keep encouraged,
Missing me one place search another,
I stop somewhere waiting for you.

In this poem the world the 'I' finally inhabits is remarkably elemental. 'I' is left with the 'spotted hawk', the 'last scud of day', the 'air', the 'sun', the 'dirt', and the 'grass'. These final circumstances may remind us that 'Song of Myself' is trying to enact Emersonian Transcendentalism in which, according to Emerson's 'The American Scholar' (1837), 'nature is the opposite of the soul, answering to it part for part'. In the opening poem of 'Song of Myself' this belief is dramatised in the lines: 'I loafe and invite my soul, / I lean and loafe at my ease observing a spear of summer grass.' Communion with the soul and communion with nature are in these lines, as they are in Emerson, mutually reflective activities. They are Transcendental activities in that they assure the self of its participation in a divine transcendence which also sustains the objective world of nature. As the opening poem goes on to claim, the harmony thus established between the soul and nature confers on the individual self 'perfect health' and 'original energy'. It is in this redeemed state that the poet claims to be delivering to us the exemplary 'Song of Myself', his 'original energy' being energy from the origin of things – in other words, the energy of Creation.

As 'Song of Myself' begins, so it might be said it ends. In the final poem, the self is resigned to its ultimate diffusion into a process which includes the self but always moves beyond it. This process and the self's inclusion in it are wonderfully evoked in the fourth to the eighth lines of the poem. Such lines are unimaginable as coming from a contemporary English poet. For English writers the world remained unperceivable without what James called its 'attendant forms'.[3] Here, we have an American self and its world with no forms intervening, the very expression of the case being in verse which itself is 'free' of structural aids and determinants. There is in the lines a mood of profound resignation as the self consents to give itself up: 'I depart', 'I effuse', 'I bequeathe'. All it now has left as a demonstration of its powers is a self-mocking gesture: 'I shake my white locks at the runaway sun'.

This mood of reconciliation with the end is a matter of Whitman's Transcendental ideology which we may choose to take or leave. The point I want to make at this stage is how precariously close to its denial the ideology for Whitman always stood. Referring to the sun earlier in 'Song of Myself', he had written: 'Dazzling and tremendous how quick the sunrise would kill me, / If I could not now and always send sunrise out of me' (25).[4] After the first line here, how necessary for mere survival is the instant ideological bravado of the second. Wordsworth's sun, in Book II, lines 181–93 of *The Prelude*, can be reassuringly accommodated in the 'attendant forms' of reflective blank verse and familiar settings: 'I had seen him lay / His beauty on the morning hills'. Whitman's reminds us of the ultimate hostility of the primal world towards man experienced by another American consciousness in *Moby-Dick*. Similarly, in the elemental world in which the self is finally left in the last poem, we have Ahab-like forebodings of annihilation, oblivion and inconsequence which the Transcendentalism must counter.

Such forebodings threaten Whitman's proclaimed function as the poet of democracy who is in instant contact with his readers, delivering to them what they are more than ready to hear. In the second line of 'Song of Myself' we are told: 'And what I assume you shall assume'. In the final poem, however, we read: 'I too am untranslatable, . . . / You will hardly know who I am or what I mean, . . . / I stop somewhere waiting for you'. These lines may still be full of assurance. In this light they look forward to the poem 'Shut Not Your Doors' (1866), in which Whitman insists: 'The words of my book nothing, the drift of it everything'. His poetry, so he is claiming, is 'original energy', having a force beyond what is implied to be the mere clothing of its language.

Less assuredly, Whitman is also recognising in the above lines from 'Song of Myself' his possible ineffectuality and insignificance. In the elemental space of the New World in which even at the end of the poem he is still left, what mark has he made? What recognition of his consequence has he gained from 'the runaway sun'? The boastful complacency behind his proclaimed fellowship with the 'spotted hawk' is surely matched by the anxiety of needing to claim this additional identity for the self, after so many others have already been voiced in the work as a whole. Despite a 'Song of Myself' lasting for fifty-two poems, the self is still unassured, waiting for the reader in a 'somewhere' which may as well be nowhere.

As is clear from the other writers in this book, the achievement of authorial identity, voice, or perspective was something nineteenth-century American writers found very problematic. The elemental New World, as it is evoked in the poem above, gave no helpful clues. nor did it give any clues to the related problem to do with the identity and whereabouts of the reader. 'Song of Myself', therefore, in contrast to *The Prelude*, cannot be the pronouncements and reflections of a narrator confident that his educated sensibility will find its counterpart in the reader. Its precariousness in this respect is a condition of its being. It is a product of the doubt, shared by other nineteenth-century American writers, that subjectivity would ever find a confirming objectivity. Transcendentalism was one way of attempting to resolve this doubt. It pronounced the subjective to be objective and the objective to be subjective. It enabled Whitman to give a voice to America in the third quarter of the nineteenth century, and to hope to be identified with what he voiced. He wanted his America to be a 'Song of Myself'. Yet, as poem 4 tells us, the self remained always: 'Both in and out of the game watching and wondering at it', belonging as much to an unlocated private world as to a public world. As for the public world, the Civil War confirmed momentously that its potential for instability and disintegration more than matched this potential within the self.

II

'To be in any form, what is that?' (27), asks Whitman at the mid-point of 'Song of Myself'. The question brings to mind Hamlet's famous question: 'To be, or not to be'. In this context it is not unreasonable to take *Hamlet* as an exemplary type of Old World literature, in which the hero's life is wasted by a combination of his sense of his own and the world's corruption, together with bad news from the past. It belongs to the New World spirit of 'Song of Myself' that the self should not be troubled by Hamlet's despairing alternative to being. Nor, so the rhetoric of the following lines insists, need any ghost from the past undermine the possibilities of the present:

There was never any more inception than there is now,
Nor any more youth or age than there is now,

And will never be any more perfection than there is now,
Nor any more heaven or hell than there is now.

(3)

Reacting against this New World discarding of history, and in this respect following Hawthorne and James, Eliot was to claim in 'Burnt Norton' (1935): 'If all time is eternally present / All time is unredeemable'. For Whitman, life is redeemed because the eternal is realised in the present. As he puts it in poem 23: 'Endless unfolding of words of ages! / And mine a word of the modern, the word En-Masse'. In the New World the unfolding of eternity has at last fulfilled itself by delivering the present of America. The condition of all men and women in this 'now' is ideal and equal: 'I speak the pass-word primeval, I give the sign of democracy' (24).

One of the determinations of 'Song of Myself' is to name, and give free verse acclaim to, the multifarious aspects and lives of the United States. At the beginning of the 1855 Preface to *Leaves of Grass* it is asserted that 'the United States themselves are essentially the greatest poem'. The ideal of the nation, that is to say, exists already in reality. All the poet is doing ('the words of my book nothing') is delivering it into its inevitable language:

All truths wait in all things,
They neither hasten their own delivery nor resist it,
They do not need the obstetric forceps of the surgeon.

(30)

The poet is delivering the truth of America as the recovered paradise, where evil, in Emerson's words from 'The Divinity School Address' (1838), 'is merely privative, not absolute: it is like cold which is the privation of heat.' Evil is not an inevitable ingredient of the self's fundamental being and of the systems of life itself. As in the case of the confined woman in poem 11, it is only the stultified or neglectful loss of 'perfect health'. Similarly, when life has gone wrong on the larger public scale, as in the graphic account of the massacre of the Texas Rangers in poem 34, this bad news from the past is recorded so that it can be contained and transcended in the recovered 'now' Whitman is celebrating. There is a determination not to see such events as, in Coleridge's ominous words from 'Kubla Khan' (1816): 'Ancestral voices prophesying war'.

It is easy to be dismissive of Whitman's proclamation of a New
World and to accuse him of mere blindness to the facts of life.
What should make us hesitate from such simple responses is the
sense we have of Whitman's conscious adoption of a role. Later he
was to characterise himself, 'As Adam early in the morning' (1860).
This kind of self-consciousness ('*As* Adam') permeates 'Song of
Myself'. He is disarmingly frank, for example, about the symbol
which was to live in his imagination for a lifetime of poetry:

> A child said *What is the grass?* fetching it to me with
>   full hands,
> How could I answer the child? I do not know any more
>   what it is than he.
>
> (6)

What follows in this poem is a series of optimistic guesses, the
implied challenge being, that if we do not know the meaning of
grass, let alone life, why assume the worst? 'Magnifying and
applying come I', he writes later:

> Lads ahold of fire-engines and hook-and-ladder ropes no
>   less to me than the gods of the antique wars,
> Minding their voices peal through the crash of destruction,
> Their brawny limbs passing safe over charr'd laths, their
>   white foreheads whole and unhurt out of the flames.
>
> (41)

There is no doubt here that he is self-consciously talking life up, as
elsewhere he talks himself up: 'Walt Whitman, a kosmos, of
Manhatten the son, / Turbulent, fleshy, sensual, eating, drinking
and breeding' (24). It can be said against 'Song of Myself' that, as in
the case of the above firemen, it repeatedly presents a day-dream
world of excitement in which the mindless monotony of much of
the world's work, presented unforgettably in 'Bartleby the Scri-
vener' (1853), is never recognised. Yet, as Conrad shows in *Heart of
Darkness* (1902), when the colonial naval powers shell unseen
natives in the African jungle because these natives have been
termed 'enemies', reality is determined frequently by the language
we use. Change the language, so the thesis of 'Song of Myself' has
it, and you not only change the reality, but bring into being a better
reality that was always potentially there. In this redeemed world it

would not be the case that jobs would be allowed to entail a loss of humanity. A human being would not, in Emerson's words from 'The American Scholar', be 'metamorphosed into a thing' and be worth only his or her function. With this thesis Whitman is voicing a still pertinent attack on a continuing injustice:

> Many sweating, ploughing, thrashing, and then the chaff for
>   payment receiving,
> A few idly owning, and they the wheat continually claiming.
>
>   (42)

What an insight into the modern condition is provided by the line, 'And mine a word of the modern, the word En-Masse'. How appropriate, since the condition is of world scale, the foreign language term is. In the world of the modern, with its questioning of hierarchical structures, what will the meaning of the universal 'en-masse' in its multifarious guises be? Whitman's democratic idealisation of the United States (and eventually of the whole world in 'Passage to India' (1868)) is a determined attempt to declare that the place has structure and coherence and is not the expression of anarchic appetency. Throughout his career, however, his commitment to the organic actuality of the democratic New World, which his poetry was merely delivering into language, was poised precariously against the desolating knowledge that he was making it all up. Indeed the recourse to notions of organic form, which in the American scene we also find in Emerson, Thoreau and Melville, was a product of the necessity to believe in something, when other plots and structures for the mass of mankind (such as Dickens could still hang on to) were not felt to pertain. In the early twentieth century, with the crowd flowing over London Bridge in *The Waste Land* (1922) and wandering round Dublin in *Ulysses* (1922), there was an equivalent recourse to myth.[5] The note of desperation we occasionally hear in 'Song of Myself', as in the worked up rhetoric of poem 41, signals the burden Whitman has on his hands. Throughout 'Song of Myself' and *Leaves of Grass* as a whole, it is felt that the United States are the final expression of life's possibilities. The implication is that the expression had better be good. To fall short of the ideal in the New World is, after all, to be left nowhere. History has institutionalised neither the complacencies of compromise and failure, nor what might pass for their wisdom.

The sense of finality in 'Song of Myself' is confirmed by the absence in it of the possibility of development. Although the poem is full of motion and activity, paradoxically it is going nowhere. In this respect it is like *Huckleberry Finn*, another song of an American self, wherein the ever-changing 'I' is in and out of the game and on a journey which is not a journey, or which at least has no destination. In both works the implication is that what humanity can make of itself, it now has made. Manifestly, Twain is not favourably impressed by the result, though he can always continue to amuse himself with a joke. Slavery alone in *Huckleberry Finn* gives the lie to any claims the United States might make to being a redeemed New World.

Whitman can weave the ideal song of the self even from the facts of slavery:

> I am the hounded slave, I wince at the bite of the dogs,
> Hell and despair are upon me, crack and again crack the
>   marksmen,
> I clutch the rails of the fence, my gore dribs, thinn'd
>   with the ooze of my skin,
> I fall on the weeds and stones,
> The riders spur their unwilling horses, haul close,
> Taunt my dizzy ears and beat me violently over the head
>   with whip-stocks.
>
> Agonies are one of my changes of garments.
>
> (33)

With *Huckleberry Finn* in mind, it is worth noting that these lines present a more graphic account of the viciousness of slavery than anything we find in the novel. Even so, there is nothing abolitionist about them, or about other scenes of slavery in poem 15. As the last line confirms, they concentrate rather on including the plight of the fugitive slave within the completeness of 'Song of Myself'. It is as if Whitman, even with material of this kind, is only intent on demonstrating what he can do as an American poet. Later he is to ask: 'Would you hear of an old-time sea-fight?' (35). He wants to show us the identities he can adopt, the scenes he can depict, the range American poetry has.

All significant art is to a large extent display and changes of garment, and must, therefore, frustrate the non-artist's simpler notions of sincerity. We may still conclude nonetheless that, with respect to slavery, an absolute evil, display and changes of garment point to 'Song of Myself' as being morally and politically useless. As will be the case with the Civil War, it is as if Whitman's containment of conflict within the imagination is the equivalent of its containment in reality. Again we arrive at the sense that outside the poem there was for Whitman no reality. With no ordaining and historical structure to have recourse to, only the imagination is holding the United States together against all the forces (slavery being one) which are pulling it apart.

No wonder Whitman writes: 'Do I contradict myself? / Very well then I contradict myself' (51). His contradictions are more than the inconsistencies and changing positions of any long life. They are the expression of a nineteenth-century American self whose only counter to a context of indeterminacy, in which the self and the United States can be anything or nothing, is a determined proclamation of identity and transcendent design. The proclamation is incessant, because although 'Song of Myself', like *Leaves of Grass* as a whole, is going nowhere, it is at the same time without stasis. The present disappears as soon as it happens. Even from poem 5, with its beautifully controlled realisation of Transcendental experience, the self passes on. This poem is full of confident assertion about the equality of soul and body and their loving relationship. It has no doubt about the self's harmony with God and the whole world, for 'a kelson of the creation is love'. Yet the experience justifying the confidence was in the past, and there is no certainty that it will return or continue to sustain. As from 'A Squeeze of the Hand' in *Moby Dick*, we move on. On the journey to nowhere which diffuses all proclamations, the experience will never again be recalled. There will be no point of stasis from which to have recall.

In these pioneering circumstances Whitman, in Pound's words, 'broke the new wood' of language. From Pound's poetic predilections between 1910 and 1914 when he wrote these words in his poem 'A Pact', one suspects it was the bare, direct accuracy of Whitman's free verse that impressed him. In 'Song of Myself' I am thinking, for example, of the vivid and tactile realisation of the men's bodies in poem 11. Such lines are something new in the language, as are the lines reporting the massacre of the Texas Rangers and the account of the sea fight in poems 34–6.

Whitman is justly famous for his single line word pictures of the

New World's countless activities.[6] In addition, and in contrast, to depictions of unceasing motion, there are unforgettable lines enacting natural, peaceful well-being:

> I lean and loaf at my ease observing a spear of
>   summer grass
>
> (1)

> The air tastes good to my palate
>
> (24)

Whitman could make words collide against, and qualify, one other in surprising combinations:

> Who goes there? hankering, gross, mystical, nude.
>
> (20)

He 'broke the new wood', because he was as Adam, untrammelled, freshly naming the New World as it happened, proclaiming the self's place in a transcendent cosmic harmony, dreading the self's aloneness in an eternal cosmic void.

III

Between the polarities of harmony and void Whitman found no middle ground. This is why, like other nineteenth-century American writers, he has next to nothing to say about day-to-day individual conduct, or personal and social relationships. Usually, relationships in his poetry are no more than occasions for ideology. As in 'I Saw in Louisiana a Live-Oak Growing' (1860), they too are likely to become an expression of the self's fundamental need not to be overwhelmed by its sense of solitariness 'in a wide flat space'.

Because the polarisation is unchanging, there is no development in Whitman. His poetic career is not a matter of an optimistic, 'innocent' beginning, which is transformed, as it might have been by the Civil War, into a more doubtful, 'experienced' end. Neither a reading of his poetry in the order in which it was written, nor a reading of it in the 'Clusters' or groups in which, from the 1860 *Leaves of Grass*[7] onwards, the poems were arranged, supports any developmental view. As my treatment of 'Song of Myself' has indicated, Whitman, even in the 1855 *Leaves of Grass*, and despite the claims of its Preface, was already aware that the United States were not the greatest poem, in the sense of being a manifestation of a harmonious New World. This antithesis to the thesis is confirmed by other poems in the first *Leaves of Grass*.[8]

In 'The Sleepers' the self is imagined wandering all night in its visions: 'Wandering and confused, lost to myself, ill-assorted, contradictory'. In one of these visions the very ideal of Whitmanesque, heroic maleness, 'a beautiful gigantic swimmer swimming naked through the eddies of the sea', finds that nature is not the opposite of the soul, when the waves break his 'beautiful body' on the rocks and eventually bear away his corpse. Whitman's recording of life's violation of his most idealised figures, as in the case of the Texas Rangers in 'Song of Myself', is remarkable for a poet whom Feidelson, in a representative way, has claimed 'does not really believe in the possibility of wreck'.[9] It is as if his imagination of disaster, which always countered his imagination of the ideal, has already prefigured what would happen to Lincoln.

The hostility of nature towards humankind is equalled only by the violent conflicts humankind itself engenders. In the case of the founding of the New World, these involved war with Britain and the dispossession of the aboriginal inhabitants. A vision of the 'blanch'd' and defeated Washington at Brooklyn, viewing 'the slaughter of the southern braves confided to him by their parents', is a reminder of the cost of the former. More haunting, is the unresolved legacy of the latter. In the remarkable section 6 of 'The Sleepers', the poet remembers a story told by his mother, 'Of when she was nearly a grown girl living home with her parents on the old homestead'. Suddenly, one morning they were visited by a 'red squaw':

My mother look'd in delight and amazement at the stranger,
She look'd at the freshness of her tall-borne face and full
    and pliant limbs,
The more she look'd upon her she loved her,
Never before had she seen such wonderful beauty and
    purity.

As is usual in Whitman, gender in these lines is no more than nominal. The 'she' could as well be 'I'; the red squaw a red brave. Even with so noble a savage, however, there will not be the reconciliation the white imagination longs for. The same afternoon the squaw departs, 'nor was heard of there again'.

What does reconcile the conflicts in 'The Sleepers' is not the daytime world so much of 'Song of Myself' celebrates, but the night-time world of sleep. Sleep and night are the only maternal embrace the orphaned, Oedipal male self (such a continuing presence in nineteenth-century American literature) will ever find. Already in 1855, they are a prefigurement of the ultimate reconciling embrace of mother death, to which 'Out of the Cradle Endlessly Rocking' (1859), 'Scented Herbage of My Breast' (1860) and 'When Lilacs Last in the Dooryard Bloom'd' (1865–6) are to sing famous praises. This prefigurement is confirmed by the poem 'To Think of Time'. Beginning in part 4 with a naturalistic treatment of a funeral which is equivalent to parts of the treatment of Dignam's funeral in *Ulysses*, the poem goes on to declare:

If all came but to ashes of dung,
If maggots and rats ended us, then Alarum! for we are betray'd,
Then indeed suspicion of death.

This 'Alarum' is dismissed in the poem's conclusion: 'I swear I think there is nothing but immortality!'

Earlier in this essay, I talked of Whitman's journey to nowhere. It was in fact always a journey to death. 'Hoping to cease not till death', he writes in the first poem of 'Song of Myself'. As in *Arthur Gordon Pym, Moby-Dick*, Dickinson's poems and *Huckleberry Finn*, death is the only end, because there is no other end on the way. No other end provides a structure of life by which experience might be appraised, ordered and settled. This is why experiences in nineteenth-century American literature are often like beads on a string, random encounters in an ocean, or chance villages on a river bank, having hardly even a sequential relationship. Until death, life is a perpetual going forth, or lighting out for new territory. As Whitman writes in the last line of 'There Was a Child Went Forth': 'These became part of that child who went forth every day, and who now goes, and will always go forth every day.'

'These' are all its experiences. For the most part the poem realises vividly an ideal of an American childhood, in which the subjective self is at one with the objective world. Between the self and the world nothing intervenes. As might have been the case in the Garden of Eden, the function of language becomes simply one of naming:

> And grass and white and red morning-glories, and white and red
>   clover, and the song of the phoebe-bird,
> And the third month lambs and the sow's pink-faint litter,
>   and the mare's foal and the cow's calf,
> And the noisy brood of the barnyard or by the mire of the
>   pond-side,
> And the fish suspending themselves so curiously below there,
>   and the beautiful curious liquid.

The poem has moments, especially to do with the 'mother' and the 'father', which any reactionary sentimentalist would endorse. Richard Chase said well that 'the feeling [Whitman] exhibits in praising domesticity is one of the many indications that in his sentiments and, indeed, in his profoundest emotional disposition Whitman was conservative and nostalgic.'[10] This conservatism and nostalgia, however, are the projection of an ideal stability which it is the representative American fate, as realised by the poem, never to rest on. Instead, there is the obligation forever to go forth, one experience always displaced and discounted by the next, until all experience is rendered transient and ungraspable, and selfhood is never established. Although the first half of the poem is delivered in the past tense as if the voice of the poem, as in several English first person tales, has arrived at a point from which to look back, there has been no such arrival. Nor, so the last line indicates, will there ever be. The second half of the poem becomes a present tense, and in the last line all tenses, past, present and future, are one. To refer to Eliot again, all time in this poem is eternally present and, by the end of the poem, there are signs that for Whitman too this eternal present is felt as an unredeemable burden. The voice of the poem is left without a perspective and a structure for the experience it delivers, just as the child is left without a perspective and a structure for the experience it lives. This is why the child, in so far as it has an identity aside from the process of its experience, eventually remains, like Twain's Huck, always a child. No structure of adulthood is imaginable as an achievable end. The only end is 'The horizon's edge, the flying sea-crow, the fragrance of salt-marsh and shore mud'.

It is the unreachable end, which is not an end, faced at the conclusion of 'Song of Myself' and to be faced many times again. 'You up there walking or sitting / Whoever you are, we too lie in drifts at your feet': so concludes 'As I Ebb'd with the Ocean of Life' (1860). 'You' is the gods or the audience; 'we' the poet and his fellows, who are seeking an end or an audience which will be the confirmation of significant identity and life. In 'Facing West From California's Shores' (1860), 'very old', but still a 'child', he was to ask: 'But where is what I started for so long ago? / And why is it yet unfound?' The very title of this poem in the American context is breathtaking. Unless death was an end which made sense of it all, Whitman was wrecked indeed.

IV

Meanwhile, he was repeating himself in too many of his poems. The 1855 *Leaves of Grass* could have done without 'A Song for Occupations', 'I Sing the Body Electric' and 'Song of the Answerer'. From the 1856 edition no one would miss the loss of 'Salut au Monde!', 'Song of the Broad-Axe' and 'By Blue Ontario's Shore'. 'Starting from Paumonok' could have been advantageously omitted from the 1860 edition. While 'Song of Myself' has the 'original energy' of a genesis, these poems are redundant declamations and assertions of the same material, only readable by a dogged act of will. In them Whitman's thesis that everything happening can be seen as the expression of a beneficent transcendent design for the self and the world is so unrestrained it makes no sense.

As I have said, the thesis was never to change, not even in *Drum Taps*, the series of poems published in response to the Civil War. In these poems the thesis continued to remain significant, as it would in some post-Civil War poems, because it was experienced as a projection against its haunting antithesis. What this means in *Drum Taps* is that the war is seen as a stage in the United States' heroic development in order to prevent its being seen as the nation's disintegration into chaos. To maintain this view, Whitman evades the actual issues of the war and refrains from supporting or denouncing either side. Several poems are an exhilarated call to participation in war as such. In the last part of 'Rise O Days From Your Fathomless Deeps', for example, it is revealed how the self

has been 'Hungering, hungering, hungering, for primal energies
and Nature's dauntlessness'.

But now I no longer wait, I am fully satisfied, I am glutted,
I have witness'd the true lightening, I have witness'd
    my cities electric,
I have lived to behold man burst forth and warlike America rise,
Hence I will seek no more the food of the northern solitary wilds,
No more the mountains roam or sail the stormy sea.

As also in 'Song of the Banner at Daybreak', the war has become
the occasion for the individual's and the nation's full self-
realisation. It is to the war, therefore, that the child in the latter
poem must now go forth. Not to rise to this moment of history is to
miss the essential life, the 'manly life in the camps', to which, in
'First O Songs for a Prelude', so many are seen downing tools and
running, as in a series of frames from a movie.

As the pre-war poems might have led us to expect, there is an
element of wilfulness, evident in the near frenzy of 'Beat! Beat!
Drums!', in this view of the war. M. Wynn Thomas, in a comprehensive and stimulating response to *Drum Taps*, goes so far as
to find a 'Whitman frustrated by a society permeated by material-
ism, to the point where he passionately wishes to see it cleansed by
violence and forcibly regenerated'.[11] 'Must I indeed learn to chant
the cold dirges of the baffled? / And sullen hymns of defeat?'
Whitman asks in 'Year that Trembled and Reel'd Beneath Me'. His
determination to see the Civil War as the extreme throes of his
nation's birth, and not as internecine conflict, is his imagination
pressing back against the threatened annihilation of all his hopes.
The pictorial quality of 'Cavalry Crossing a Ford', therefore (along
with that of 'Bivouac on a Mountain Side', 'An Army Corps on the
March' and 'By the Bivouac's Fitful Flame'), is as a composed scene
on Keats's Grecian Urn. An actuality is captured, but deprived of
cause and effect (Why is the calvary crossing the ford? Where has it
come from? Where is it going? Is it Northern or Southern?). The
result is that the event is removed from a potentially disturbing
context to become a scene in the impersonal and transcendent
process of history. The same is true of the wounded, depicted with
graphic horror in 'A March in the Ranks Hard-Prest and the Road
Unknown' and in 'The Wound-Dresser'. They are representative
wounded in history's design.

The end of the design, so Whitman wants to believe, is transcendent 'Reconciliation':

Word over all, beautiful as the sky,
Beautiful that war and all its deeds of carnage must in time
    be utterly lost,
That the hands of the sisters Death and Night incessantly softly
    wash again, and ever again, this soil'd world;
For my enemy is dead, a man divine as myself is dead,
I look where he lies white-faced and still in the coffin – I
    draw near,
Bend down and touch lightly with my lips the white face in the
    coffin.

In this brief poem Whitman is consciously exposing his whole
faith, even as he expresses it, to the possibility that it may be no
more than a contrivance of words. He is in the characteristic
American position of having no structure outside the work itself to
authorise the relationship of even one line to the next. Of the first
two lines, which is cause and which effect? 'Beautiful that' may
mean 'with the result that'. In this case the statement in the first
line is the cause of the effect in the second line and indeed the
third. 'Beautiful that', however, may also mean 'in that' or 'because'.
If this were the meaning of the phrase, the second line and
the third would be the cause of the effect of the first.

   Beyond themselves and the meanings they try to make, the
words have very little public or objective guarantee of their authority
other than the assertion that the sky is 'beautiful', and the
implication that 'Death and Night' are as the sea washing 'this
soil'd world'. As a result, the 'I' within a Whitman poem is again
left, without the possibility of resolution, in a starkly polarised
position: 'For my enemy is dead, a man divine as myself is dead'.
The 'For' beginning this line is another ambivalent conjunction.
Can the statements it introduces be made, because there is a 'Word
over all'? Or is there a 'Word over all', because these statements
can be made?

   Even the line itself is self-questioning. If the man is 'divine as
myself', how can he be 'my enemy'? Alternatively, if the man is
'my enemy', which one of us, if either, is divine? Whatever assertive
confidence there seems to be in the second half of the line is
undercut by an equal amount of doubt.

To borrow terms from *Moby-Dick*, the 'I' has attempted to strike through the mask. What was thought to be the enemy is dead. Yet the mask of otherness remains on the white face, finally unreachable as enemy or lover. Whatever the 'Word' is which would authorise the identity of self, the nature of otherness and their mutual reconciliation, is unrevealed.

V

If there was a final word for Whitman, it had already been revealed in 'Out of the Cradle Endlessly Rocking' (1859) and in 'Scented Herbage of My Breast' (1860). It was to be confirmed in 'When Lilacs Last in the Dooryard Bloom'd' (1865–6). As the first of these poems discovers orgasmicly, it was the 'word final, superior to all', the word: 'death, death, death, death'. This word, as I have shown, was already implied in 'The Sleepers'.

'Death' has its place and function in 'Reconciliation', but the fact that it is not identified as *the* word is evidence of how provisional Whitman's arrival at even a 'final' word always was. Matthiessen noted famously that Whitman described *Leaves of Grass* as 'only a language experiment'.[12] This phrase suggests what the poems confirm, that words for the New World are unceasing, since the experiment of the New World apparently has no end. In these circumstances, the pressure to find a word, which would be an end and a meaning, becomes all the more unremitting. As James was to put it, 'The American world produces almost everywhere the impression of appealing to any attested interest for the word, the *fin mot*, of what it may mean.'[13] 'Death', undoubtedly, can be seen as the last word and as the ultimate reconciling democracy. But what a defeat of Whitman's hopes for America, as represented in the daylight world of 'Song of Myself', this particular last word signifies. The earlier poem had refused to accept even death as an end to America's vital expression of itself. It had declared: 'The smallest sprout shows there is really no death' (6).

In 'Crossing Brooklyn Ferry' (1856) Whitman offers the crossing of rivers by ferry as a kind of last word, in that he sees it as an ultimate unchanging activity, uniting humanity throughout all time. Despite the impressive evocation of crossing the river in the second paragraph of part 3, I find the affirmed faith to be achieved too easily in this poem. 'Crossing Brooklyn Ferry' does not have the close encounter of affirmation with negation which is a condition of Whitman's best poetry. In part 6 of the poem, for example, the 'I' reveals that it too has had its setbacks in life: 'It is not upon you alone the dark patches fall'. What follows by way of support for this claim, however, lacks personal pressure (Whitman was never very good at realising an internal self) and is entirely formulary. The equivalent passage in part 2 of 'As I Ebb'd with the Ocean of Life' is more convincing because it is doubting the very affirmative self Whitman seeks to proclaim. One would like to know in 'Crossing Brooklyn Ferry' what the consequences of some of the misdeeds were and who got hurt. Instead we have something approaching the fatalistic banality of the popular song 'My Way'.

I find myself, as Lawrence found himself often with Whitman,[14] resisting the inclusive claims made for the experience in 'Crossing Brooklyn Ferry'. The complication of similarity but difference is too easily avoided. It could only be avoided successfully when the experience confronted was so elementally a question of the nature of our existence, as to be fundamental to humanity. So, in 'Out of the Cradle Endlessly Rocking', we have the realisation, inspired by the bird, that our life may be an inconsequential passage through a loveless world to the fearful incomprehensibility of death. To counter this void the poet wants to get beyond the merely personal, merely egotistical, claim on life which the bird is making. Life on the bird's terms can only lead to desolation, for sooner or later what one loves will always be taken away. The birds were 'only living' and, as Eliot puts it in 'Burnt Norton': 'that which is only living / Can only die'. 'Out of the Cradle Endlessly Rocking' wants to get beyond this condition to a transcendent sense of life and death.

Whitman's poems about the sea recall Shakespeare's last plays, themselves set against the sea's awesomeness. 'Did you not name a tempest, / A birth and a death?' asks Thaisa at the end of *Pericles*. In the last plays, Shakespeare too is reaching beyond the personal to a faith in processes which are as eternally creative as destructive. So, in 'Out of the Cradle', the sea is a 'fierce old mother', a 'savage old mother', but nonetheless a mother. We are nurtured even by the energy which insists insidiously on our death. Personal alienation is resolved into a transcendent union of beginning and end.

Reconciliation and continuance in Shakespeare's last plays are realised in the marriage of children of the next generation. Even the impersonal, therefore, retains a personal quality. In Whitman's poem, however, the self remains as alone in its consolation as in its desolation. The consolation has no human face, and is part of no human scheme of things, even though the sea is assertively greeted as 'mother'. As often in Whitman, one wonders if the consolation derives from anything other than assertiveness. In itself, the consolation is the expression of an egotism which, if more sublime than the bird's, remains egotism.

In 'Out of the Cradle Endlessly Rocking', the self is singing a 'reminiscence'. Later, 'Song for all Seas, all Ships' (1873) begins with the line: 'To-day a rude brief recitative'. There will always be other reminiscences, other recitatives, because there is no relationship between the self and the world, other than what the poems must continually voice. Indeed there is no self, other than what the poems must continually voice. In the remarkable opening paragraph of 'Out of the Cradle', so inseparable from its experience is the self, and so barely containable is the experience, that identity for the self has no more substance than the first person pronoun.

'When Lilacs Last in the Dooryard Bloom'd' seems to contrast with 'Out of the Cradle Endlessly Rocking' in that it is full of scenes of American life. Like most of such scenes in Whitman's poetry, these too are an attempt to declare into being an instant America. Hawthorne wrote of the 'visionary and impalpable Now, which, if you once look closely at it, is nothing'.[15] So, for Whitman (with especial horror after the Civil War and the assassination of Lincoln) the 'Now' of all his hopes for America could seem as nothing. Whatever was in place was, after all, so insubstantial. In part 14 of 'When Lilacs Last', in a line which wonderfully registers the New World, Whitman writes of 'the large unconscious scenery of my land with its lakes and forests'. Put this line alongside phrases from *The Prelude* such as 'my darling Vale' and 'this earth / So dear' (Book II, lines 202 and 438–9) and one gets a sense of what Whitman means by 'unconscious'. In the New World it is the imagination ('Pictures of growing spring and farms and homes') which must instantly create the consciousness, the *reality*, unprovided by any attendant, substantiating forms from the past.

What the imagination projects in the poem is a vision of an America that will always survive its tragedies, the particular tragedy of the assassination of Lincoln and the more general tragedy of the Civil War. That these tragedies are deeply felt cannot be doubted. In part 2 we have the personal exclamation of utter despair, in part 15 appalling memories of the war:

I saw battle-corpses, myriads of them,
And the white skeletons of young men, I saw them,
I saw the debris and debris of all the slain soldiers of the war.

The 'I' within the poem wants to keep a hold on its grief, even while it responds to the recurrent rebirth of life as announced by the 'Ever-returning spring'. As in *The Waste Land*, not to be aroused by the spring would be a privation equalled only by the inability to mourn what has been lost. To have neither desire nor memory is ultimate destitution, only to have either one is an anodyne, while to be impelled by both may be a disabling contradiction.

Cutting across and interpenetrating this complication is the problem, amid death's endless recurrence, of paying especial tribute to Lincoln's death and the deaths of all the slain soldiers. Everything (lilac, star, the bird and the coffin) presses for attention at the same time. By its very being, the poem is realising a sense of life in which every aspect of experience exists simultaneously and always. The 'I' is therefore attempting to create a structure where there may be none. It wants to claim the death of Lincoln as a unique moment, signalled when 'the great star early droop'd in the western sky in the night'. In part 8 we read, 'O western orb sailing the heaven, / Now I know what you must have meant as a month since I walk'd'. The 'must' here is striking. It recalls the poet's admission in 'Song of Myself' that he did not know the meaning of grass. Again we have an advertisement of the imagination's imposition of meaning. The Transcedentalist proposition that the world is symbolic and can be read by the imagination for its absolute meaning proves untenable.

In any case, even the imposed meaning was, as meanings usually are, in the past. Meanwhile the cycle of life and death is unceasing. In the midst of life there is always death: 'Over the breast of the spring, the land, amid cities, . . . / Night and day journies a coffin'. When it is not Lincoln's coffin, it is someone else's and will eventually be our own. Whitman's obsession by death, his sense of its annihilating imminence, is the confirmation of how provisional and insubstantial he felt life to be. I know other writers have asserted 'Life's but a walking shadow' (*Macbeth*, V.v.

24), but the provisionality and insubstantiality I find in Whitman pertain particularly to the so illusory American life presented in this poem and elsewhere. So unsustained by it is the 'I' in 'When Lilacs Last', that like other fugitive voices in American literature he too 'fled forth to the hiding receiving night that talks not'.

Here is another way of describing what *Huckleberry Finn* will finally call 'the Territory ahead'. That territory could only be death, probably as meaningless as the life (the talk) the fugitive was fleeing. Not that Whitman will settle for meaningless death. As in 'Out of the Cradle', the destroyer is hymned as the creator. The tomb is a return to the womb. After a lifetime of alienation in what *Moby-Dick* proclaims to be a 'stepmother-world' (Chapter 132), the loving embrace of mother death awaits. The proposition enables the 'I' of 'When Lilacs Last' to affirm of the corpses of the Civil War:

They themselves were fully at rest, they suffer'd not,
The living remain'd and suffer'd, the mother suffer'd,
And the wife and the child and the musing comrade suffer'd,
And the armies that remained suffer'd.

It is something to say, after what for Whitman had been the greatest of wrecks.

6

Dickinson's Poetry

For no other writer in this book does the search for the identity of the self in America assume the intensely concentrated form it assumes in Dickinson's poetry. None of the others is as unrelievedly absorbed in the mystery of self as she is. To begin my demonstration of these points, I shall look first at poem 528:[1]

> Mine – by the Right of the White Election!
> Mine – by the Royal Seal!
> Mine – by the Sign in the Scarlet prison –
> Bars – cannot conceal!
>
> Mine – here – in Vision – and in Veto!
> Mine – by the Grave's Repeal –
> Titled – Confirmed –
> Delirious Charter!
> Mine – long as Ages steal!

This poem can seem impenetrably private. As with many of Dickinson's poems, it is not even clear what its tone should be. Does it have an exulting voice, or a voice of calm deliberation? It is about possession, but what is possessed is unknown or cannot be stated. Nor can it be made clear by what right something is possessed. 'White Election', 'Royal Seal' and 'Scarlet prison' look and sound as if they each have an objective, public meaning, but they haven't.

The poem expresses the apparent paradox that the act of saying 'Mine', which is a separating act, claims its validation from commonly agreed rights or signs. Personal possession, in other words, is upheld by public codes or laws. In this respect, it can be said that even possession of the self (the subjective) must be confirmed by the world (the objective).

Does it then follow that if there is no self that can be defined, there is no world that can be defined, no subjective, no objective? I think this is a question the poem is enacting. The poem asserts possession, but it cannot even say it is the self which is possessed. Nor can the poem establish its world in shared, public terms.

As we might expect from an American writer, this is very American writing. The dashes in Dickinson's poetry are not eccentricity. They signify the blankness of the unknown (What *is* mine? What *is* the world?) and the space between propositions. As is the case with other writers in this book, Dickinson cannot assume that one proposition made by language (one word, one phrase, one poem, one episode, one chapter) will self-evidently lead to another. She is writing without the support of sustaining forms which have an objective validity. For her, as for other American writers, the question, after any initial proposition, must essentially have been: 'What comes next?' What, other than a dash, comes next, and what comes after the dash?

Where her terms do suggest a public meaning (for example, 'Election' and 'Grave's Repeal'), the meaning has been subverted or disconcertingly transformed. 'Election' clearly has its roots in New England Calvinism with its belief that God had elected those he would save and those he would damn – but 'White Election'? As for 'Grave's Repeal', while it might have belonged to an affirmation of life beyond the grave, the way the phrase is placed in this poem leaves such an affirmation fighting for survival.

We are faced in the poem with disjunctions rather than junctions: with 'White' against 'Scarlet'; 'here' against 'Vision' and 'Veto' and 'Grave's Repeal', but with none of these last three terms being synonyms. We are faced with affirmed possession which has also to do with prison and deprivation. Gain is loss: '*Mine* – long as Ages *steal*' (my emphasis).

'Delirious Charter!': are not all charters (including this poem) 'delirious' when we are deprived of shared coherences? Unless 'I' can share rights of possession with 'You', I can possess nothing, not even myself, for there is nothing to possess.

What is finally remarkable about this poem, as about so many of Dickinson's, is its impersonal quality. Its emphatic personal force, in other words, derives from its presentation of a dramatic voice enacting its condition.

More obviously impersonal is poem 303:

> The Soul selects her own Society –
> Then – shuts the Door –
> To her divine Majority –
> Present no more –

Unmoved – she notes the Chariots – pausing –
At her low Gate –
Unmoved – an Emperor be kneeling
Upon her Mat –

I've known her – from an ample nation –
Choose One –
Then – close the Valves of her attention –
Like Stone –

Dickinson habitually writes in a considering tone in which she is detached from what we might consider to be parts of the self. Along with 'The Soul' (also in 512), there are, for example, 'The Nerves' and 'the stiff Heart' (341) and 'This Consciousness' (822). In the above poem we might be tempted to equate the self and the soul. One gets the sense, however, that the soul is being assessed, presumably by a part of the self which is not the soul. One part of the self, therefore, is judging what we might call another part of the self and is indeed at odds with it. It may be that the first part of the self, the voice of the poem, is, or would like to be, more gregarious and spontaneous, less imperious and wilful. We cannot know much about this first part of the self, since it is only minimally implied by its response to the soul. As is usually the case with Dickinson, the voice of the poem pronounces the poem out of nowhere.

The voice of the poem is in awe of the soul, but it is an awe betraying doubtful resignation as much as admiration. Part of what is being allegorised and assessed in the poem is the cost of presumption and exclusivity. It is a subject Dickinson returns to, as we shall see, in poems 326 and 379. The presumption and exclusivity might be only personal qualities. They could also be religious, moral, or political. Whatever their particular nature, the soul's imperatives are seen to be as negative as they are positive. To be 'Unmoved' by what attends one, even unmoved by a kneeling 'Emperor', is undoubtedly a kind of supremacy. Like Bartleby's attempted supremacy to all contingency in Melville's story, however, it is a supremacy belonging as much to death as to life.

The presentation of the soul in this poem is contrary to what we find in Emerson, Thoreau and Whitman. In this connection, Dickinson's poem may be helpfully compared with poem 5 of 'Song of Myself'. In Whitman's poem, the unity and harmony of soul and body, self and world, subject and object, are also the Transcendental oneness of God and all creation. Whitman is confidently familiar with 'my soul', but in Dickinson's poem 'The soul' is its own force, as much other from whatever is the self, as part of whatever is the self. It is given a female gender, and this may indicate that it has to do with whatever it is that determines gender and the sexual ramifications. Even in this respect, however, it remains (as gender and sexual forces do) mysterious and even alien, only knowable in its imperatives. To all inquiry it is as unyielding and unrevealing as the 'stone', to which it is finally likened, but from which it might have been thought to be so different.

Dickinson is often compared to the English metaphysicals. Though she is more unrelievedly abstract than they are and never as full of the world, this poem is evidence of the aptness of the comparison. Seeming opposites come together. 'Like Stone –' arrives with an inevitability after the coldness of 'selects' and 'Unmoved', and after the chillingly vivid (and very sexual) 'close the Valves of her attention'. Valves suggest both the organic and the mechanical. They prepare for 'Stone' by intimating something both of, and apart from, nature. The seeming inevitability of the arrival at 'Stone' is also aided by the poem's astonishing economy and vividness. So much of the pageant of life is suggested by the middle stanza. It is as if whole worlds are passing by.

Again we see Dickinson's ability to enact and consider at the same time. The dashes play an important part in pacing the poem and ensuring words and phrases receive appropriate attention. I have suggested there is an inevitability about the poem, but it should be recognised that this inevitability is only sensed after the event of the poem. As one reads it, one is rather aware of the poem finding, making, considering itself as it goes along. This undetermined quality is another effect of the dashes. It is especially noticeable at the beginning of the poem, before and after 'Then'. Momentarily, it is as if the voice of the poem does not know what comes next. What it does eventually say seems only part of other things that might be said. The final word, as the last inconclusive dash indicates, will never be said.

The soul can be observed in its present ('selects'), known in its past ('I've known her'), but the future is '–'. Where does this leave the 'I' of the poem, the voice of the poem? The answer is, in the nowhere from which it began the poem. 'I' is barely separable from a process, an energy, of the soul which it cannot know and cannot

control. 'I', therefore, cannot know itself and remains uncharac-
terised. It is as dispossessed as the voice in the previous poem
which cannot say what is 'Mine'.

Dickinson returns again and again to her sense that the self can
only be experienced and observed in its divisions, or as part of
something other than the self, and, therefore, may never be a
knowable or possessable entity. It is this problem which is dramatised and considered in the much discussed poem 754:[2]

> My Life had stood – a Loaded Gun –
> In Corners – till a Day
> The Owner passed – identified –
> And carried Me away –
>
> And now We roam in Sovereign Woods –
> And now We hunt the Doe –
> And every time I speak for Him –
> The Mountains straight reply –
>
> And do I smile, such cordial light
> Upon the Valley glow –
> It is as a Vesuvian face
> Had let its pleasure through –
>
> And when at Night – Our good Day done –
> I guard My Master's Head –
> 'Tis better than the Eider-Duck's
> Deep Pillow – to have shared –
>
> To foe of His – I'm deadly foe –
> None stir the second time –
> On whom I lay a Yellow Eye –
> Or an emphatic Thumb –
>
> Though I than He – may longer live
> He longer must – than I –
> For I have but the power to kill,
> Without – the power to die –

I see this poem as a dramatisation and consideration of the self's
relationship to its life and its death. As in poems 465 and 510,

Dickinson often writes as if life and death, or intimations of life and death, are happening to the self without its control. In the above poem she is exploring the fact that the self's life and death are of the self and also other than the self. The self does not choose to live and therefore does not choose its life. There is a sense in which the self's life can be said to wait, like a Fate, for the self to be identified with it. This proposition is implied in the poem's first stanza. Who identifies the self with its life, who is the 'Owner', is finally an unanswerable question. Once beyond infancy, the self may feel it identifies itself with its life. Yet there always remains the sense that the self is not entirely its own 'Master'. It is not absolute or autonomous. 'Me' is always the self and something that may not be the self. It is always more than one force, as much 'We' as 'Me'.

The self's life waits for the self as 'a Loaded Gun', full of dangerous potentiality. One of the striking things about the poem is that it envisages the self's life mainly in terms of violent energy and conflict. The self hunts. It guards. It is a 'deadly foe', with 'the power to kill'. In this respect the poem shares a mood of Dr Johnson's when, commenting on a moment in *Richard II*, he writes: 'It is a matter of very melancholy consideration, that all human advantages confer more power of doing evil than good.'[3]

From the second to the fourth stanza the poem is indeed a mixture of triumphalism and regret. It is full of the sense that the achievement of any one life is always at the expense of other, perhaps more fulfilling, lives that might have been lived. The penultimate stanza has a tragic quality. In it the self may be performing greatly for any of the greatest of causes. When it comes down to it, however, what a reduced, jaundiced life even the great performance may be, merely the movement of an 'emphatic thumb', pressed as it might be now-adays on the nuclear button.

The fact that the 'Owner' is referred to as 'Him' and as 'Master' gives rise to the argument that what the poem is specifically enacting is the female life and death, perverted in unavoidable subservience to male domination. In this respect the poem might be compared to poems 246, 461 and 732. The first of these begins: 'Forever at His side to walk – / The smaller of the two!' Just as the self guards 'My Master's Head' in the above poem, so poem 246 goes on to speak of bearing forever the largest part of his grief. Female and male rela-tionships in Dickinson's poetry are never presented as relationships of equals. The last phrase in the fourth stanza above is tinged with profound regret and longing. Dickinson does not write: ''Tis better than the Eider-Duck's / Deep pillow to have shared'. By using the dashes to separate '– to have shared –' from the sentence of which the phrase is part, she undermines the triumphant affirmation of subservience the sentence at one level wants to make. The phrase thus expresses a powerful desire for a more equal relationship than the self has ostensibly settled for.

The last stanza, it can be argued, reveals the awareness of the female self that masculine systems will always outlive it. In poem 461 such systems stretch even into 'Eternity'. At this stage, however, I want, as a man, to get myself back into the poem in a role other than that of villainy. I want to see the poem's enactment and consideration of the self's relationship to life and death as not pertaining only to one gender. The gender of the voice of the poem is in fact not specified, and it would make no difference if 'Master' became 'Mistress' and the masculine pronouns became feminine pronouns. Life stands as 'a Loaded Gun' as much for a man as for a woman. What 'a Loaded Gun', for example, in Shakespeare's play, *Antony and Cleopatra* are to each other.

As I try to understand the puzzling last stanza, I am reminded of the wonderful, tragic encounter in Chaucer's 'The Pardoner's Tale' between the three young men and the old man. Dickinson's poem enacts the positions of Chaucer's poem at this stage, the young men wanting to conquer death, the old man wanting 'the power to die'. The energy released in most of Dickinson's poem can be seen as young energy, trying to forget it will ever die, all its life an attempt to triumph over death and thus separate life from death. Even at the end ('Though I than He – may longer live'), there is a forlorn hope that the self will conquer death. This hope is overtaken by the knowledge that our very life is one with our death, and that 'He', the process of life and death, our 'Owner' and our 'Master', must indeed outlast us. Then our position may well be that of Chaucer's old man and of the self at the end of Dickinson's poem. There remains 'the power to kill'. As in the old man's case, we can still send the young to their deaths. Our own death, however, remains a visiting stranger, happening to us, mastering us, as our life has happened to, and mastered, us.

Our end waits, as our beginning waited, stopping for us, as another famous poem (712) puts it, because we cannot stop for it. 'Without – the power to die –' also implies without the power to live. It is as if whatever is the essential 'I' remains untouched by either its life or its death. This condition of being is again enacted in 'I heard a Fly buzz – when I died –' (465). At the end of that poem the 'I' is left without a life or a death. What was its life has been discounted in the bleak, though resilient, ironies of 'Keepsakes' and 'Assignable'. What is its death is: 'and then / I could not see to see –'. All that remains is what Melville terms 'the intense concentration of self',[4] the representative American state of being castaway, in the face of life and death.

II

My interest in Dickinson is not biographical. It is the imaginative life of her poems I find compelling, not her 'legend', however that legend is understood. I am not sure what different (let alone better) kind of life, which might not have occasioned her particular poems, or any others, we should retrospectively wish for her. Her own poem about the poet argues for the impersonality of the poet's talent (it is another force which the self may experience but which does not belong to the self) in a way Eliot, in 'Tradition and the Individual Talent' (1919), would have supported:

> This was a Poet – It is That
> Distills amazing sense
> From ordinary Meanings –
>
> (448)

The poet's talent is 'That'. The creative act is past tense as soon as it is finished, in that the poem is then outside the self, indifferent to the self. It will have, as poems 290, 883 and 1261 reveal, its own afterlife. Nor can the re-acquaintance of 'That' and the self be guaranteed: 'Your thoughts don't have words every day' (1452).

Dickinson's interest for us now is 'That'. Adrienne Rich has described it as, 'engaged in a lifetime's musing on essential problems of language, identity, separation, relationship, the integrity of the self; . . . capable of describing psychological states more accurately than any poet except Shakespeare.'[5] Though this concluding judgement may exaggerate, the significance of the 'musing' as described in the first part of the quotation is indubitable. It is not the expression of a peculiar, deprived woman. Many of her poems, as is the case with the one we began with, are not gender specific, while her lines, 'And I, and Silence, some strange Race / Wrecked, solitary, here –' (280) might be an epigraph for the voices of several of the texts in this book. In this American scene, in which the 'Silence' provided no confirming objectivity, the self was always a mysterious arena of irrepressible and irresolvable divisions. 'I felt a Cleaving in my Mind –' (937) writes Dickinson with her characteristic dramatic directness. Poe, Hawthorne, Melville, Twain and James were familiar, in their different ways, with the resulting world of nightmare and madness her poetry frequently presents, not as an excursion from normality, but as normality itself. 'I maintain', Poe wrote, 'that terror is not of Germany but of the soul'.[6] Dickinson puts it thus:

> One need not be a chamber – to be Haunted –
> One need not be a House –
> The Brain has Corridors – surpassing
> Material Place –
>
> (670)

The poem goes on to discount the horrors of the Gothic excursion: 'Ourself behind ourself, concealed – / Should startle most –'.

The concealed self, never in its American way settling for public territory, appears again in the following poem:

> I cannot dance upon my Toes –
> No Man instructed me –
> But oftentimes, among my mind,
> A Glee possesseth me,
>
> That I had Ballet knowledge –
> Would put itself abroad
> In Pirouette to blanch a Troupe –
> Or lay a Prima, mad,
>
> And though I had no Gown of Gauze –
> No Ringlet, to my Hair,
> Nor hopped to Audiences – like Birds,
> One Claw upon the Air,
>
> Nor tossed my shape in Eider Balls,
> Nor rolled on wheels of snow
> Till I was out of sight, in sound,
> The House encore me so –

> Nor any know I know the Art
> I mention – easy – Here –
> Nor any Placard boast me –
> It's full as Opera –

(326)

This poem is about a state of dispossession becoming paradoxically and dangerously a state of possession. It is not clear if the speaker wanted but could not get instruction, or if the speaker refused instruction. There is regret as well as defiance in the opening two lines, and 'instructed' is especially ambivalent. It can mean both 'ordered' and 'taught'. The self may be wise to refuse to be ordered. It may not be wise to refuse to be taught.

The otherness of things as they are, which any self must come to terms with, is signified for the female self of this poem by 'Man'. The self has two possibilities: to try to be a star under man's instruction, on the world's terms, like a 'Prima', or to be a star on its own terms, 'among my mind'. Either life for the self is a role. In this poem, as in others, neither the subjective nor the objective life has an absolute reality. Only in a role can the self, the 'I', become aware of itself.

Which role should the self settle for? The 'I' in the poem cannot answer this question, and the poem reaches no conclusion. On the world's terms, the self might have had acceptability, dressed in its public role ('Gown of Gauze'), performing like a petted animal ('hopped to Audiences – like Birds'). That way may lie humiliation for the self, even violation. But then the reward for withdrawal 'among my mind' may be an equal humiliation, an equal violation:

> But oftentimes, among my mind,
> A Glee possesseth me,

Compensation for being deprived of the world's acclaim becomes possession by one's own fantasies. In the mind is the self-delusion of there being no impossibility or forbidden territory. Everything to the self-flattering mind is 'easy' to 'mention'. It has secret powers: 'Nor any know I know the Art'. It is the arena of powerful, vindictive, all-conquering passions: 'lay a Prima mad'. It always plays to its own packed house: 'full as Opera'.

In poem 379 what the self creates for itself in its own theatre is even more ominous:

Rehearsal to Ourselves
Of a Withdrawn Delight –
Affords a Bliss like Murder –
Omnipotent – Acute –

We will not drop the Dirk –
Because we love the Wound
The Dirk Commemorate – Itself
Remind Us that we died.

It is not clear whether the self has had a delight withdrawn, or whether it withdraws wilfully with its own delight. Either way, the poem registers the thrill of the self's autonomy. Why does the self need connections outside the self, when it can omnipotently rehearse 'a Withdrawn Delight' to such exciting effect?

The third line is the answer to this question, in that it makes a comment on the kind of 'Bliss' 'Withdrawn Delight' becomes. The 'Murder' can be both self-murder and murder of any relationships beyond the self. Paradoxically, 'Withdrawn Delight' becomes ultimate self-violation and ultimate violation of what is other than the self.

The voice of the poem is inclusive and suggests that if the experience were ours we may have the awareness 'that we died'. This awareness is not certain, hence the subjunctive 'Remind' in the last line. With this form of the verb the poem's final statement becomes a plea: 'Let it remind us', or 'May it remind us'.

The poem confirms that Rich's association of Dickinson with Shakespeare is not extravagant. Its enactment of the self-punisher in love with the rehearsal of self-inflicted wounds is a perfect gloss on, say, Leontes in *The Winter's Tale*. Eventually, Leontes is rescued. What will be the fate of the voice of the poem? It is very difficult to separate its dramatic enactment of the condition it presents from comment on that condition. This is because the voice of the poem only just manages to get itself outside the experience of the poem. It is not sure it has been, or can be, rescued from further rehearsals, hence its final plea. It is as if the last line is an attempt by the voice of the poem to put the experience behind it and arrive at a saving judgement. Unless it can do this, it has no way of distinguishing 'Withdrawn Delight' from any other delight, or 'Bliss like Murder' from any other bliss. It is trapped within the theatre of the self, where all values are self-serving.

We often find the self in a Dickinson poem in reflective soliloquy, as if it were a character playing for high stakes in the middle of a Shakespeare play:

> Mine Enemy is growing old –
> I have at last Revenge –
> The Palate of the Hate departs –
> If any would avenge
>
> Let him be quick –

                                                              (1509)

Poem 401 speaks contemptuously of 'Gentlewoman'. It is as if the voice of the poem were at the side of the stage, watching them walk by and commenting on them to us:

> What Soft – Cherubic Creatures –
> These Gentlewomen are –
> One would as soon assault a Plush –
> Or violate a Star –

There is a tone here reminiscent of Richard III or Iago, two of Shakespeare's surrogates for the artist as villain. Interestingly, there are no thoughts of equal violence towards men. Undoubtedly, 'gentlewoman' is not an identity Dickinson would want for the self.

Nor, as far as the poems reveal, would she want to call the self 'wife'. Her several poems about wives (187, 199, 246, 461, 732, 1072, 1737) reveal no advantage in this title, except that 'It's safer so –' (199). 'How many times these low feet staggered –' (187) contemplates a dead housewife and the pathos of her life's work. Her only release from a lifetime's chores is her death. Her enemies remain unvanquished:

> Buzz the dull flies – on the chamber window –
> Brave – shines the sun through the freckled pane –
> Fearless – the cobweb swings from the ceiling –
> Indolent Housewife – in Daisies – lain!

One reason for the profound effect of these lines is their avoidance of sentimentality. The lines mock the housewife as much as they mourn her. The cobweb has a kind of gaiety as it swings from the ceiling. It can have been no fun being a spider in this housewife's domain, even though the spider, as Eliot reminds us in 'Gerontion' (1919), will never 'Suspend its operations'. The last line is unforgettable. 'Indolent Housewife', in the world's eye, is a contradiction in terms. To be indolent is not to earn the title housewife, and because this housewife has earned her title, she may never till now have lain in daisies. Now, however, she is dead and so separate (note the dashes) from the living flowers. What might have been Whitman's Transcendental organicism ('The smallest sprout shows there is really no death' ('Song of Myself', poem 6)) is its denial. There is death, and this housewife, 'Brave' and 'Fearless' in her battles (these words may well apply to her as well as, respectively, to the sun and the cobweb), is finished. In the first two stanzas she is as inanimate as something made out of metal. The final line of the poem is closed, not left open with a dash.

Whatever relationship the self desires with another in Dickinson's poetry is frustrated. The desired relationships range from the possibly sexual, certainly passionate, 'Wild Nights' (249) to the reasoned 'That I did always love' (549). Of the latter, it might be claimed that only the dashes and the final word, 'Calvary', distinguish it from what might be a voice and argument of Donne. The claim would be true, except that it is characteristic of Dickinson that the other party to the relationship is never actualised. The consequence is that even the celebrated 'I cannot live with You –' (640) makes rather an abstract meal of itself.

As Gelpi has said, 'in several poems it is impossible to identify "him" as lover, death, or Christ'.[7] I first read the breathtaking poem, 'Till Death – is narrow Loving –' (907), as an account from the woman's point of view of a relationship (probably as wife) with a man. The poem is a miniature novel, and I saw it as a compressed summary of how a woman may be held till death in the system of a man's narrow loving, her whole 'privilege' of life wasted. The 'He' of the poem, however, may well be God, while the voice of the poem has no specific gender. However we settle these issues, if we need to settle them at all, the existence realised in the poem's last two lines is awful to contemplate. It is the self's final condition that it

> Delight of Nature – abdicate –
> Exhibit Love – somewhat –

How the dashes again control our arrival at the words and phrases! 'Delight of Nature' has a Blakean authority as an absolute value, and the poem makes us feel it as a perversion that 'Delight of Nature' should need to abdicate. Similarly, it is a perversion that the first two words of the last line should ever function together.

Such a poem demonstrates that although in Dickinson the 'other' in a relationship remains as abstract as in Whitman, the terms and consequences of relationships can have an actuality in Dickinson which they do not have in Whitman. This kind of actuality reminds us of C.G. Rossetti and E.B. Browning, though its manners are not as developed in Dickinson as in the work of these English poets. Whitman and Dickinson are more comparable in their intimate realisation of nature:

> Through the Dark Sod – as Education –
> The Lily passes sure –
> Feels her white foot – no trepidation –
> Her faith – no fear –
>
> Afterward – in the Meadow –
> Swinging her Beryl Bell –
> The Mold-life – all forgotten – now –
> In Ecstasy – and Dell –

(392)

I am not persuaded this poem is part of Dickinson's imagining 'an apocalyptic day of resurrection on which women would rise from the grave of gender in which Victorian society had buried them alive, and enter a paradise of "Ecstasy – and Dell –"'.[8] The lily is personalised here only to realise how impersonal, and consequently how other, it really is. For the voice of the poem, 'Education' has been more than 'the Dark Sod'. This voice has felt, and feels, 'trepidation' and 'fear'. It cannot forget. While Dickinson does not believe in Whitman's Transcendental view of nature, the above poem shares a recurrent human mood with some lines of his. I am thinking of his teasing pronouncement: 'I think I could turn and live with animals, they are so placid and self-contain'd' ('Song of Myself', poem 32). The mood is a momentary desire to escape the complications of our humanity. It is an admiration for living things which seem complete unto themselves, with no concern for consequences. In Dickinson's poem, only the poet and the reader, not the lily, have to think what comes after that final dash.

Despite an intimacy with nature which becomes direct address in poems 1035 and 1320, and despite a claim that in the 'Orchard' she is going 'to Heaven' 'all along' (324), Dickinson's most abiding sense of the self's relationship with nature is found in poem 1333:

> A little Madness in the Spring
> Is wholesome even for the King,
> But God be with the Clown –
> Who ponders this tremendous scene –
> This whole Experiment of Green –
> As if it were his own!

This poem (especially the fourth and fifth lines) might have been by the early Stevens of *Harmonium* (1923). Later, in his more discursive manner, Stevens was to write: 'we live in a place / That is not our own and, much more, not ourselves'.[9] For both Dickinson and Stevens, belief in the Transcendental harmony of the self and the world, avouched by Emerson, Thoreau and Whitman, was unsustainable. In the 'Introduction' to *Nature* (1836) Emerson affirmed: 'we have no questions to ask [of Nature] which are unanswerable'. In 'Answer July –' (386), however, nature itself in its annual cycle can only pose questions, not answer them. In so far as we are part of nature's process, our lives are not glorified in the way that Emerson, Thoreau and Whitman sought to maintain. Rather, as in poem 342, they are depersonalised and merely ritualistic:

> It will be Summer – eventually.
> Ladies – with parasols –
> Sauntering Gentlemen – with Canes –
> And little Girls – with Dolls –

How easy in this stanza, and in the rest of the poem, Dickinson can make it seem to write perfectly! What a difference there is between 'It will be Summer eventually' and what she actually writes. Desperate to prove his creative energy, Whitman boldly declares in poem 25 of 'Song of Myself':

Dazzling and tremendous how quick the sun-rise would kill me,
If I could not now and always send sun-rise out of me.

Dickinson has conceded in this contest. She has already, as one poem puts it frankly, and with a characteristic humour which makes us love her undeceiving sense of the self, 'got my eye put out' (327).

III

'Forever – is composed of Nows –' (624), Dickinson announces. None of her more than 1700 poems is a major occasion in the developing stages of a poet's life. They are instant variations on repeating themes. Their voices live in that unstructured American present, also occupied in their different ways by the narrative voices of Poe, Whitman, Melville and Twain. 'This visionary and impalpable Now, which, if you once look closely at it, is nothing'[10] was what Cooper, Hawthorne, James and, later, Eliot, explicitly tried to get a perspective on in their search for history. As Eliot was to put it in 'Little Gidding' (1942), 'A people without history / is not redeemed from time'. Dickinson ('A Day! Help! Help! Another Day!' (42)) was in Eliot's sense unredeemed. A reason for her repeatedly writing about death was that it might provide a perspective on a continuing present, having no end but death:

> Behind Me – dips Eternity –
> Before Me – Immortality –
> Myself – the Term between –
> Death but the Drift of Eastern Gray,
> Dissolving into Dawn away,
> Before the West begin –
>
> 'Tis Kingdoms – afterward – they say –
> In perfect – pauseless Monarchy –
> Whose Prince – is Son of None –
> Himself – His Dateless Dynasty –
> Himself – Himself diversify –
> In Duplicate divine –
>
> 'Tis Miracle before Me – then –
> 'Tis Miracle behind – between –
> A Crescent in the Sea –
> With Midnight to the North of Her –

And Midnight to the South of Her –
And Maelstrom – in the Sky –

(721)

This poem returns us to poem 528 at the beginning of this essay. In it, the self is without definition, except that it exists as something for some period of time. The period of time ('the Term between') cannot be defined. Nor can it be certain that 'Myself' and 'the Term between' (note the dash) are to be identified. The 'Term between' may always exist whether the self exists or not. When any self exists, however, there will be a 'Term between' unique to it.

To ask 'Between what' is to ask an unanswerable, even an ungraspable, question. We have no reliable language by which the question might be explored. 'Behind' and 'Before', for example, can both mean the same thing. They can both mean what preceded 'Me' and what follows 'Me'. Similarly, 'Eternity' and 'Immortality' can have identical meanings, whatever the meanings are.

As the poem sees it in the first stanza, therefore, the self exists between undefinable time in a motion of things which, in the last three lines, is also undefinable. The beautiful evocation of the dawn in these lines again brings together meanings and connotations which we might expect to stay apart: 'Death', 'Dawn'; 'Eastern', 'West'. The lines present a traditional religious position in which death is also a new beginning, a new dawn. There is, however, immense scepticism in the presentation. 'Drift' and 'Dissolving' are without reassuring effect, while the last word, followed by a dash, is another of Dickinson's subjunctives hanging in a space.

The scepticism is continued into the middle stanza, where there is an attempt to imagine the Christian orthodoxy of transcendent life after death. The attempt occasions incredulity, the formulary words begetting only themselves, signifying nothing.

The beginning of the last stanza echoes the beginning of the first, with the relationship of 'before', 'behind' and 'between' similarly unsettled, while 'Eternity' and 'Immortality' have now collapsed into 'Miracle'. The word, 'between', leads to 'A Crescent in the Sea', and it is not certain what relationship this phrase has to 'Me', just as earlier it was not certain what relationship 'the Term between' had to 'Myself'. 'A Crescent in the Sea' may evoke the moon reflected in the sea, or the crescent of a wave in the sea. Whichever, we have again the impalpable nature of what is 'between'.

We might feel we learn something of what is between in the poem's last three lines. With the word, 'Her', we now at least have gender. Even this minimal definition, however, may be no more than a token. If it begs the question (and it does) to define immortality in the middle stanza in masculine terms, it also begs the question to define existence in this life in female terms. Gender is another concept this poem deconstructs. 'Me' and 'Myself' in the poem are of undefined gender and could be either or both. The last lines of the poem may be echoing Tennyson's 'The Charge of the Light Brigade' (1855), with its 'Cannon to the right of them / Cannon to the left of them'. If there is an echo, its purpose is certainly to offer female heroism as a counter to Tennyson's celebration of masculine heroism. More than that, however, its purpose is also to show that any self could be in either of the representative situations in the two poems. To make either situation gender specific is always to short-circuit the question of the meaning of the self. In Dickinson's poem the self has all before it.

Or is nothing 'Before' it, 'Behind' it, 'North' of it, or 'South' of it? In the poem the New World self cannot be defined, and wherever the self is cannot be defined. The self, without form, is in the presence of great energy, 'Maelstrom', without form. Such is Dickinson's representative American scene.

7

Twain: *Adventures of Huckleberry Finn* (1884)

> You don't know about me, without you have read a book by the name of 'The Adventures of Tom Sawyer,' but that ain't no matter. That book was made by Mr Mark Twain, and he told the truth, mainly.[1]

Huckleberry Finn's presentation of Mark Twain recalls Arthur Gordon Pym's presentation of Edgar Allan Poe. In both these American books, it is the narrator who tells us about the author. Fiction is ascendant. The narrator of *Huckleberry Finn* introduces himself not by reference to a real world in which he might be supposed to live, but by reference to a previous story. As for 'Mr Mark Twain', that is an entirely fictional identity.

The opening sentences of *Huckleberry Finn* exemplify again in nineteenth-century American literature the tendency of the imagination, uncertain of its relationship to reality (or 'truth') to become self-sustaining. While the relationship of imagination and reality is never without its complications in any culture, it was made more problematic in the American scene by the absence or irrelevance of the Old World conventions by which it had long been negotiated. This extra burden on his authorial compatriots is what James is discussing when, in Chapter 2 of his book *Hawthorne* (1879), he produces his list of all the things American civilisation lacks, for example:

> . . . no aristocracy, no church, no clergy, no army, no diplomatic service, no country gentlemen, no palaces, no castles, nor manors, nor old country houses, nor parsonages, nor thatched cottages nor ivied ruins.

In English culture all these items belong as much to imagination as to reality. Consequently, one's imagination of, say, a castle may be a close match to what one can actually find. There is a memory bank of conventional images, concepts and literary forms, because reality has as long been possessed and structured by imagination as imagination as been possessed and structured by reality. Such a state of affairs provides rich pickings for the writer. To use material such as James has in mind is to exploit realities which have already been organised in the reader's imagination in relationship to all sorts of other realities.

The absence of established demarcations in the New World, either in reality or the imagination, is reflected in the unsettled, nearly lawless, literary forms of *Arthur Gordon Pym*, *Moby-Dick*, *Leaves of Grass*, Dickinson's poems and *Huckleberry Finn*. When formal settlement is achieved, as in Poe's shorter pieces and in Hawthorne and James, there is a marked tendency towards the artificial. Imagination is imposing itself on reality rather than inhering in it.

Artificiality of this kind is evident in some of the ingredients of *Huckleberry Finn* and is one of the themes of the book. While it has a king and a duke, together with military and country gentlemen in the persons of Colonel Grangerford and Colonel Sherburn, these personages are not the real thing. The obvious histrionic and parodic quality of the king and the duke extends to the performances of the two colonels, costumed in their white suits. As is the case with Tom Sawyer, who longs in the New World for adventures among 'palaces' and 'castles' such as are on James's list, the roles these figures create for the self remain unconfirmed by the reality they inhabit. Paraphernalia from the Old World, even Hamlet's 'To be, or not to be' soliloquy, 'the most celebrated thing in Shakespeare' (Chapter 21), become ludicrous or even dangerous in the New.

Not to have sustenance from the past, however, is to face the New World unaided, deprived of the securities by which life has been shaped. When Huck is separated from Jim in the fog, we read:

> I kept quiet, with my ears cocked, about fifteen minutes, I reckon. I was floating along, of course, four or five mile an hour; but you don't ever think of that. No, you *feel* like you are laying dead still on the water; and if a little glimpse of a snag slips by, you don't think to yourself how fast *you're* going, but you catch

your breath and think, my! how that snag's tearing along. If you think it ain't dismal and lonesome out in a fog that way, by yourself, in the night, you try it once – you'll see.

(Chapter 15)

Melville's gloss on such a representative New World experience of the self as 'The Castaway' is found in the chapter of that name in *Moby-Dick*: 'The intense concentration of self in the middle of such heartless immensity, my God! who can tell it?'

The author and all the major characters are castaways in *Huckleberry Finn*. The book is told in a language which, more than any other in nineteenth-century American literature, is a declaration of independence from established modes of literary discourse. Yet the language belongs nowhere in the sense that it expresses no system of values and life. As much Pap's as Huck's, it is inevitably unsettled, disintegrative, and, ultimately, fugitive. Within the fiction it makes wry and momentary contact with us, its jokes being a minimal sustenance. After the fiction, nobody knows 'the Territory ahead' (Chapter 42).

II

In other words, the American *Huckleberry Finn* is not the developing story of a young boy who eventually arrives at some kind of understanding of himself and the world. By discussing the book's structure and its narrator I want to show, in this part of my essay, that such a *Huckleberry Finn* does not exist.

Twain's book is not *Great Expectations* (1861), in which the first person narrator, at the end of his adventures, tells the story of his growth from childhood to the revelations that awaited him. In *Great Expectations* these revelations also await the reader, as Pip, the narrator, recreates for us the childhood, adolescence and young manhood of his time-past. With the older Pip we re-experience the motive, moral and plot by which time-past has become time-present. Time-past is created with wonderful vividness, but it is monitored by Pip from the end in time-present where he now is. We read towards that end.

Huckleberry Finn always frustrates our desire to assume we are *en route* to a meaningful end. At one stage it proposes an end ('to get on a steamboat and go way up the Ohio amongst the free states'

(Chapter 15)), but then it immediately abandons the proposition and eventually, by taking a runaway black slave deeper into the South, makes nonsense of it and all ends. The story takes place on the Mississippi river. The distinct stages of a journey to somewhere, might, therefore, have been marked out. Yet locale in *Huckleberry Finn* is unparticularised. The book pays little attention to changes of topography (an exception is the first paragraph of Chapter 31) and, though real places (St Louis, Cairo, New Orleans) are mentioned, they are not described or evoked. During Huck's adventures, some scenes take place on the raft, some on the shore. It is as if the various villages, however, are different aspects of the same shore. They are different settings for adventures, rather than different villages in the stages of a journey. As such, they diminish further any assumption that a journey to an end is being offered.

Twain's 'Notice' warns us that no 'motive', 'moral' and 'plot', leading to a destination, are to be looked for in *Huckleberry Finn*. His book surpasses *Great Expectations* in its immediacy and spontaneity, because it is without the perspective from the end which destination provides. Unlike Pip's, Huck's adventures are unfiltered by any self other than the one immediately involved. In this American book there is no time-past and time-present. The time of its adventures is like the time of the adventures in *Arthur Gordon Pym* and *Moby-Dick*. It is the only time – a perspectiveless continuum, offered as time-past in affectation of perspective. Only on two occasions (Huck's concluding reflection on the outcome of the feud at the Grangerfords' and on Mary Jane at the Wilks') is it even implied the narrator has an existence after his adventures.

In fact the narrator has very little existence within his adventures, if by existence we mean he is a character of some substance whose purposes have a meaning beyond their immediate function. *Huckleberry Finn* is without motive, moral and plot, because Huck never has the substance to require these things. Or, it can equally be argued, Huck cannot have a substantial identity, because there is no motive, moral and plot. Both propositions would be true, though it is impossible to say which is cause and which effect. In literature, as in life, character produces, and is the product of, the systems (the motives, morals and plots) it inhabits. No character, therefore, results in no system, just as no system results in no character.

In a representative attempt to impose an identity on Huck, Henry Nash Smith and Walter Blair have claimed that he is consistently 'a character without a sense of humour'.[2] The thesis is that *Huckleberry Finn* is told as a development of the deadpan manner in which the teller pretends not to get the jokes. Huck, it is claimed, genuinely does not get the jokes. This argument can be extended to the proposition that Huck is after all an innocent boy.

Even within the first three paragraphs of *Huckleberry Finn*, however, we cannot decide if Huck is conscious or unconscious of the implications of his statements. His remark that 'a dollar a day' is 'more than a body could tell what to do with' suggests he may be a rather unconscious and innocent young boy. Similarly, it may be that we, but not Huck himself, are to get the joke in these lines: 'Tom Sawyer, he hunted me up and said he was going to start a band of robbers, and I might join if I would go back to the widow and be respectable.' In the next paragraph, however, he describes life at the widow's in these words: 'When you got to the table you couldn't go right to eating, but you had to wait for the widow to tuck down her head and grumble a little over the victuals, though there weren't really nothing the matter with them.' This remark, like many later ones (about Emmeline Grangerford's drawings and poetry, for example), has to be a deliberate and conscious joke by Huck. He must know the widow is saying prayers. The deadpan manner, therefore, is assumed.

The contradictory implications of many of Huck's statements and actions, combined with his insubstantiality as a dramatic presence, always makes it impossible even to infer a consistent identity for him. The haphazardness of his commitment to Jim is not accounted for, nor is he given the consciousness of one who, when he uses lies to manipulate others, must be as shrewd and cynical an operator as the duke is revealed to be ('If that don't fetch them, I don't know Arkansas' (Chapter 22)). Typically, such consciousness as Huck has is not enacted. The language does not draw us into him. Instead, as in the first paragraph of Chapter 5 when Huck unexpectedly encounters Pap, Huck reports on himself as he reports on external events:

I had shut the door to. Then I turned around, and there he was. I used to be scared of him all the time, he tanned me so much. I reckoned I was scared now, too; but in a minute I see I was mistaken. That is, after the first jolt, as you may say, when my breath sort of hitched – he being so unexpected; but right away after, I see I warn't scared of him worth bothering about.

Huck does have a distinct function for Twain which is of particular significance at climactic moments in Chapters 16 and 31,
when he is alarmed by the implications of his commitment to Jim.
In what has become a well known notebook entry of August 1895,
Twain described *Huckleberry Finn* as 'a book of mine where a sound
heart & a deformed conscience come into collision & conscience
suffers defeat'. Seen in these terms, Huck at these moments is the
expression of sound-heart and deformed-conscience. I hyphenate
the words because, as enacted in *Huckleberry Finn*, they are the
equivalent of composite nouns. In Chapters 16 and 31, when Huck
is trying to work out whether his commitment to Jim is good or
bad, his heart cannot be other than sound, nor his conscience other
than deformed.

He does right, but cannot think right. At these junctures his
condition is thus the reverse of what is normally human. In this
latter condition our moral sense enables us to think right, without
guaranteeing that we do right. Later works by Twain, especially
The Mysterious Stranger (1916), reveal how enraged he was by the
frequent impotence or self-contradictory results of our moral
sense. He felt humiliated by the 'Shadow' which, in Eliot's words
from *The Hollow Men* (1925), so often falls 'Between the idea / And
the reality'. Already in *Huckleberry Finn*, there is the seed of this
later position. One of the Hucks in the book will bypass the
complications and contradictions of moral sense. Endowed with
the incorruptible and intuitive goodness of a sound-heart, this
Huck, in crisis over Jim, will do good, even though his moral sense
tells him it is bad.

It is the reader who sees that the action is good. In both Huck's
crises over Jim in Chapters 16 and 31 he is obviously used ironically
by Twain. The point is that the reader should think right, with
respect to Jim and slavery, even though Huck cannot. Moral
development is thus encouraged in the reader, while it is withheld
from the narrator. This irony, which places us in a position of
superiority towards Huck, is undoubtedly a qualification of
Twain's commitment to Huck's sound-heart function at these
moments. Unlike the later Hemingway or Mailer, Twain could not
maintain an uncritical faith in the absoluteness of intuition, not
even in that of the nineteenth century's Romantic child. If 'doing
whatever come handiest at the time' (Chapter 16) could lead to a
life in harmony with nature aboard the raft, as at the end of
Chapter 18 and the beginning of Chapter 19, it could equally result

in the degradation and destitution vividly embodied in Pap Finn who, as Fiedler sees,[3] portends an ominous adulthood for a vagrant Huck. Worst of all is Colonel Sherburn's violent and wilful freedom from moral sense, when he murders Boggs in Chapter 21.

The moral enlightenment these perspectives grant the reader finds no direct expression in the book. It thus remains unendorsed by Twain. So much so, that when Huck has his second and more orchestrated crisis over Jim in Chapter 31, the episode can have the effect of being an exploitation of Huck by Twain for what by this stage is no more than an authorial performance. Abruptly thrust at us ('Once I said to myself . . .'), it is, as Poirier has claimed, 'only a re-doing of the earlier crisis' in Chapter 16.[4] As in the case of the earlier crisis, the chapters that immediately follow (at the Grangerfords' and the Phelps' respectively) are an irrelevance both for Huck's sound-heart and the reader's moral sense.

Not that we should be surprised at this result. As I have argued, *Huckleberry Finn* from the beginning has contained no possibility of development. It has not maintained a sense of an ending to which development could be leading, and there are none of the perspectives entailed by development. The book is written only to continue until it breaks off. The moments of crisis in Chapters 16 and 31, therefore, are also moments of crisis for Twain as he writes the book. Each suggests a turning-point. In an undeveloping book, they suggest development. No wonder Twain abandoned the book after the first of them in Chapter 16[5] and discounted the second with the adventures at the Phelps'.

III

I shall turn later in the essay to what all the above means for Jim. By this stage I hope I have established that Huck is more of a device than ever he is a character. Like Whitman's 'I' in 'Song of Myself', Huck enables Twain to stay 'in and out of the game' ('Song of Myself', poem 4). Poirier has recognised something of this, when he observes that 'Huck's voice is like a screen protecting the author'. Even Poirier, however, clings to what he calls 'the wondrous boy created in the first sixteen chapters of *Huckleberry Finn*'.

How far, if at all, Twain can get himself out of the game is questionable. Unlike other nineteenth-century American writers, who had Puritanism or Transcendentalism, Realism or Naturalism, to appeal to or quarrel with, Twain in *Huckleberry Finn* has nothing in the nature of a 'Big Idea' offering even the debatable prospect of a perspective. Aside from a range of superstitions, which includes notions derived from the Bible, the biggest idea in *Huckleberry Finn* is slavery. This is a dead-end which neither the characters nor the author (not even in the 1880s) want to look in the face.

In so far as Twain can get himself out of the game, it is only to become a fugitive. Consequently, there is in *Huckleberry Finn* more identification than critics usually see between the narrative voice and the other characters. Towards the widow, Tom, Pap, the new judge, Colonels Grangerford and Sherburn, the king and the duke, the Phelps and the people in the villages Twain ultimately feels neither superior nor moralistic. As they try to make sense of a place showing no more sign of motive, moral and plot than the Mississippi itself, he is too aware that their inadequacies, stupidities and confusions may be his own.

There is no belief, therefore, that anyone can become the new judge of these people and deliver a comprehending solution. Such a figure gets his come-uppance early in the book in Chapter 5. In an episode done with astonishing economy and vividness in six short paragraphs, we learn of the failed attempt of the new judge and his wife to reform Pap. It is a very funny, yet very disturbing, episode. Like most of the incidents in *Huckleberry Finn* it leaves us nowhere. We will at first be very eager not to see ourselves as the new judge. He and his wife, sentimental fools that they are, deserve everything they get at Pap's hands. Yet who wants to be left with this conclusion in Pap's debasing and anarchic corner? In so far as we ever try once more to make sense of things (even of *Huckleberry Finn* itself) are we not all new judges? Twain thinks so. By the final paragraph he has identified sympathetically with this character's point of view: 'The judge he felt kind of sore. He said he reckoned a body could reform the ole man with a short-gun, maybe, but he didn't know no other way' (Chapter 5).

Another paragraph, another joke, but this time a joke linked ominously with violence. Along with several characters in the book, Pap will die violently. The above joke portends all the violence which erupts in the book, when humour loses its momentary hold on conflict and chaos.

The feuding Grangerfords and Shepherdsons, we learn in Chapter 18, 'don't know, now, what the row was about in the first place'. Despite the humour pertaining to this situation, we should not conclude that it is all too ridiculous. Untraceable to a cause and not to be placated by sermons 'all about brotherly love', the feud is a representative enactment of our inescapable heritage of violent conflict and our predilection for violent conflict. It realises what is spoken of in 'Kubla Khan' (1797) as, 'Ancestral voices prophesying war'. Also, it is a brief American *Romeo and Juliet*, with the difference that the lovers escape and there is no sign that the families are reconciled.

It is remarkable how close to the surface the feud is. As is often the case in nineteenth-century American literature, inherent compromise, either in personal manners or public institutions, is unavailable. The chivalrous codes Colonel Grangerford invokes are manifestly an importation. Like all the manners of his household, they are applied wilfully in a vain attempt to stop things falling apart. Because these ceremonies are so artificial, the feud will be a fight to the death for a long time to come. Even the lovers must, like the narrator, become fugitive.

In the narrator himself, the immediate outcome of the feud causes his personal share of humanity's inherited guilt to well up: 'I reckoned I was to blame somehow.' It leaves him with nightmares: 'I wished I hadn't ever come ashore that night, to see such things. I ain't ever going to get shut of them – lots of times I dream about them.' In the death of Buck, who is a version of himself, his own end, perhaps equally meaningless, unreconciled, and violent, is prefigured: 'I cried a little when I was covering up Buck's face, for he was mighty good to me.'

Colonel Sherburn, another version of Colonel Grangerford, is also another possible self for the narrator. As in 'Song of Myself', the 'I' in *Huckleberry Finn* can be any of the identities to which it bears witness, because there is no inherent structure to life, establishing what the self should be. In the town Sherburn inhabits, life is barely choate:

All the streets and lanes was just mud, they warn't nothing else *but* mud – mud as black as tar, and nigh about a foot deep in some places; and two or three inches deep in *all* places. The hogs loafed and grunted around, everywheres. You'd see a muddy sow and a litter of pigs come lazying along the street and whollop herself right down in the way, where folks had to walk round her, and she'd stretch out, and shut her eyes, and wave

her ears, whilst the pigs was milking her, and look as happy as if
she was on salary. And pretty soon you'd hear a loafer sing out,
'Hi! *so* boy! sick him, Tige!' and away the sow would go, squeal-
ing most horrible, with a dog or two swinging to each ear, and
three or four dozen more a-coming; and then you would see all
the loafers get up and watch the thing out of sight, and laugh at
the fun and look grateful for the noise. Then they'd settle back
again till there was a dog-fight. There couldn't anything wake
them up all over, and make them happy all over, like a dog-fight
– unless it might be putting turpentine on a stray dog and setting
fire to him, or tying a tin pan to his tail and see him run himself
to death.

On the river front some of the houses was sticking out over
the bank, and they was bowed and bent, and about ready to
tumble in. The people had moved out of them. The bank was
carved away under one corner of some others, and that corner
was hanging over. People lived in them yet, but it was dangerous, because sometimes a strip of land as wide as a house caves
in at a time. Sometimes a belt of land a quarter of a mile deep will
start in and cave along and cave along till it all caves into the
river in one summer. Such a town as that has to be always
moving back, and back, and back, because the river's always
gnawing at it.

                                                          (Chapter 21)

The second paragraph here recalls the precariousness of the 'little
town, at the edge of the Western wilderness' in Chapter 2 of *The
Scarlet Letter*. Like the Puritans in seventeenth-century Boston
(though with no access, it seems, to their upholding sense of the
divine), Sherburn strives wilfully to establish in this town a sense
of decorum. 'A proud-looking man about fifty-five – and he was
heap the best dressed man in that town too –' (Chapter 21), he sets
a standard. To his thesis, Boggs, a modified Pap, is the antithesis.
As oppressed, presumably, as Sherburn by a sense of life's inconsequence in this place, his response is to go on 'his little old
monthly drunk' (Chapter 21) and to promote mindless commotion.
It is as if he must give the lie to the order Sherburn, or anyone else,
affects. In reaction to him the colonel becomes all the more author-
itarian and absolute: 'Till one o'clock, mind – no longer' (Chapter
21). If he stopped playing his part now, he could not live with
himself. Concession to Boggs is concession to chaos. To gun him

down in the sight of all is to resume command of centre-stage in a climactic performance: 'Colonel Sherburn he tossed his pistol onto the ground, and turned around on his heels and walked off' (Chapter 21).

The response of the narrator to the murder is to make no response, but to watch and wonder at it, and then to leave. There is, however, implicit agreement with Sherburn's contempt for the people of this town. When the mob gathers to lynch him, he faces it fearlessly and declares: 'Now the thing for *you* to do, is to droop your tails and go home and crawl in a hole' (Chapter 22). In the previous chapter, the narrator has ascribed similar Yahoo-like qualities to the people. Wanting a view of Boggs's corpse they are seen as 'squirming and scrouging and pushing and shoving to get at the window'. Watching a re-enactment of the shooting, they are represented as 'stretching their necks and listening, . . . bobbing their heads to show they understood.'

It is true that Sherburn's despair of mankind, as evinced by his speech to the lynching-party, is matched by an equal humourless-ness on his part. In *Huckleberry Finn* such a handicap as the latter might be recognised as criticism enough of any character. Other people in the town do not take the arrival of Boggs as seriously as does the colonel: 'He don't mean nothing; he's always a carryin' on like that when he's drunk. He's the best-naturedest old fool in Arkansas – never hurt nobody, drunk nor sober' (Chapter 21). People who are not Yahoos show concern for Boggs's safety. Attempts are made to get him 'to shut up'. His daughter is sent for. Sherburn murders her father, even as she arrives. On behalf of his thesis of manliness, he shoots an unarmed drunk.

These details point towards a perspective on Sherburn, but it is not endorsed by the narrator. After Sherburn has dealt with the mob and their leader, Buck Harness, we read:

> The crowd washed back sudden, and then broke all apart and went tearing off every which way, and Buck Harness he heeled it after them, looking tolerable cheap. I could a staid, if I'd wanted to, but I didn't want to.
>
> (Chapter 22)

As always, the conclusion is to leave the scene and go somewhere else. Go, in the next paragraph, as it happens, to a circus. There 'a drunk man tried to get into the ring'. With this version of Boggs the people have no patience: 'a lot of men began to pile down off of the benches and swarm towards the ring, saying, "Knock him down! throw him out!"' Fortunately, when the drunk gets in the ring and rides a horse, it is very funny. Threatened violence is transformed into laughter: 'the whole crowd of people standing up shouting and laughing till tears rolled down.' The drunk then turns out not to be a Boggs. He tears off his clothes and is revealed 'slim and handsome, and dressed the gaudiest and prettiest you ever saw' (Chapter 22).

How easily this performance could have gone disastrously wrong and perhaps in another location will do. What is it audiences want from artists, and why must artists work audiences up in these ways? With its varied cast of performers, *Huckleberry Finn* keeps up a running inquiry into the nature and function of art itself. In the New World, hierarchies of artistic convention may count for nothing. Shakespeare flops in Arkansas, but a show with the billing 'LADIES AND CHILDREN NOT ADMITTED' (Chapter 22) packs the house.

What follows is a confidence trick, but the duke is sure of the audience's response. Earlier in *Huckleberry Finn* we have had a judge who has tried, with respect to Pap, to lead the populace onto higher ground. We have also had a distinguished looking Sherburn staking a claim to be the exceptional man. Now, in reaction to the duke's latest show, we meet a new combination of these two previous figures. A 'big fine-looking man', whom Twain with marvellously delayed timing reveals to be 'the jedge', persuades his fellow 'gentlemen' to conceal how they have been duped: 'What we want, is to go out of here quiet, and talk this show up, and sell the *rest* of the town! Then we'll all be in the same boat' (Chapter 23). In *Huckleberry Finn* no title, no performance, may save us from folly or worse.

Moreover, every title, every position, every identity, is performance, and this is why the king and the duke can outbid the bluff. Their initial accounts of their talents give full rein to Twain's delightful verbal inventiveness: 'Yes, gentlemen,' the king proclaims, 'you see before you, in blue jeans and misery, the wanderin', exiled, trampled-on and sufferin' rightful King of France' (Chapter 19). We cannot believe these two believe themselves. Or can we? In the America of *Huckleberry Finn* you are what you claim you are. As is vividly depicted at the camp-meeting, a people without reason for any belief is all the more desperate to believe:

You couldn't make out what the preacher said, any more, on account of the shouting and crying. Folks got up, everywheres in the crowd, and worked their way, just by main strength, to the mourners' bench, with the tears running down their faces; and when all the mourners had got up there to the front benches in a crowd, they sung, and shouted, and flung themselves down on the straw, just crazy and wild.

(Chapter 20)

We are to see the same mass hysteria at the circus and later still at the tarring and feathering of the king and the duke:

then – here comes a raging rush of people, with torches, and an awful whooping and yelling, and banging tin pans and blowing horns; and we jumped to one side to let them go by; and as they went by, I see they had the king and the duke astraddle of a rail – that is, I knowed it *was* the king and the duke, though they was all over tar and feathers, and didn't look like nothing in the world that was human – just looked like a couple of monstrous big soldier-plumes. Well, it made me sick to see it; and I was sorry for them poor pitiful rascals, it seemed like I couldn't ever feel any hardness against them any more in the world. It was a dreadful thing to see. Human beings *can* be awful cruel to one another.

(Chapter 33)

Like the concluding reflections on Buck Grangerford's death, the final pronouncements here undoubtedly enact an inner consciousness, a deep upwelling of fear and self-knowledge that goes beyond the particular occasion. Whatever their deserts, the king and the duke are representatives now of exposed and humiliated humanity. Similarly, the victimisers are representative. All the authority of the last sentence derives from the fact that any one of us could be raging with that mob.

IV

Nothing equivalent to the reflection in the last quoted sentence is provoked by Jim's plight as a slave. Innumerable critics have shown a more conventionally moralistic and realistic concern for

Jim than *Huckleberry Finn* itself ever does. Although it is the case, as 'Fenimore Cooper's Literary Offenses' (1895) demonstrates, that Twain's only conscious theory of fiction is to do with verisimilitude and consistency, the portrayal of Jim as a fugitive black slave fails in both these respects. We cannot believe that any mature man, urgently intent on securing his own freedom and that of his wife and children, would allow himself to be involved in the adventures on board the *Walter Scott* in Chapters 12 and 13. Nor would such a man let the duke dress him up in King Lear's outfit and then paint his 'face and hands and ears and neck all over a dead dull solid blue, like a man that's been drownded nine days. Blamed if he waren't the horriblest looking outrage I ever see.' Thus arrayed, Jim, Huck tells us without a second thought, 'was satisfied' (Chapter 24).

If it is conventional realism we are looking for, we will have to acknowledge that Twain's characterisation of Jim is more inconsistent than any of Cooper's characterisations, pilloried so hilariously in 'Fenimore Cooper's Literary Offenses'. Even within a single episode, we may not be able to settle on a sense of Jim. Chapter 8, for example, ends with a minstrel show routine about speculation, initially in 'live stock'. In this routine, Jim and his fellow slaves are required to be bemused simpletons. On its own terms the routine is very funny. The last sentences, however, seem suddenly and briefly to move into different territory:

'Well, it's all right, anyway, Jim, long as you're going to be rich again some time or other.'
'Yes – en I's rich now, come to look at it. I owns mysef, en I's wuth eight hund'd dollars. But live stock's too resky, Huck; – I wisht I had de eight hund'd dollars en somebody else had de nigger.

It should be noted that the last sentence of this quotation, as established by the University of California Press text (1985), differs from what is produced in other editions. In these, the last sentence reads: 'I wisht I had de money, I wouldn' want no mo'.' Either way, the closing lines of this chapter are problematic.

The pronouncements, 'I owns mysef', and, 'I wisht I had de eight hund'd dollars en somebody else had de nigger', suggest Jim has a sudden insight into his condition. It affects us powerfully that self-ownership, a fundamental privilege of any human being, should be seen by Jim as unexpected wealth. Implicit in the pronouncement is Twain's instinctive decrying of a system which forbids large numbers of people from asserting 'I owns mysef'. This implicit denouncing of slavery is continued in Jim's final, rather forlorn wish to escape the nigger identity he has been shackled with.

Why, however, in the midst of this exchange, does Twain remind us of the immediately previous speculation dialogue, with the words: 'But live stock's too resky, Huck'? These words might suggest that even Jim's concluding remarks should be retained within the minstrel show routine. On this reading, the concluding pronouncement might become another example of Jim as simpleton, believing he could sell himself and keep the money.

Perhaps in this case Twain intends the reader, if not Jim, to appreciate the Catch 22. Also it could be argued that 'live stock' is referred to again to remind the reader that slaves were just that. The problem is Twain provides no clue as to how the final lines of Chapter 8 should be read. Nothing that precedes and succeeds them helps us with the uncontrollable variety of their possibilities. In this respect, they are typical of the way Jim is presented throughout, and it is incontrovertible that one motive for this kind of presentation is evasiveness. Whenever *Huckleberry Finn* gets close to the face of slavery, it loses itself, deliberately or carelessly, consciously or unconsciously. Irony, as in the last sentence quoted above, and as in the big performance ('All right, then, I'll *go* to hell') in Chapter 31, becomes an indulged distraction. The famous evasion chapters at the Phelps', therefore, are no more than a *tour de force* of the evasiveness which, with respect to Jim, *Huckleberry Finn* always practises.

Yet Jim is in the book. This statement of the obvious acquires significance when it is recognised there could have been a simpler *Huckleberry Finn* without him. It is not impossible to imagine a Jim-less *Huckleberry Finn*, consisting of adventures between Huck and Tom and social panorama. In several comic routines in *Huckleberry Finn*, Huck is to Jim what Tom had been to Huck in the earlier *Tom Sawyer* (1876). Jim's presence in *Huckleberry Finn*, therefore, even though his genuine force as a human being is intermittent and mainly confined to Chapters 15 and 16, is Twain's resistance to an easier book. 'What has cast such a shadow upon you?' Captain Delano asks Benito Cereno at the end of Melville's story. Jim's presence in *Huckleberry Finn* is an echo of Benito Cereno's foreboding reply: 'the negro'.

Even as we recognise that Jim does not get the end he needs, we should move on from charging Twain with evasiveness. We should begin to come to terms with what Henry Nash Smith has described as the 'latent anarchy and even nihilism' of *Huckleberry Finn*. Twain's book is not *Uncle Tom's Cabin* (1852). It has none of the latter's representative and necessary human optimism that things can be changed for the better. Unlike Stowe, Twain does not believe in redeeming anyone into the moral systems which had enslaved them, and which had deformed the conscience even of a Huck. For him, the human race once damned is always damned.

It is because *Huckleberry Finn* has no belief in absolute redeeming words that all its words are of equal value, and it is impossible for us ever to settle into an ordering relationship with the book. In fact the book in its American way embarrasses what may be a fundamentally English critical presupposition: that, of itself, the way in which words have been put together reveals their quality (even their moral quality), so that we can always discriminate between words used well and words used badly. In *Huckleberry Finn*, words present a Jim anxious for his own freedom and that of his wife and children. Later, they present a Jim who, at the behest of two boys, lets himself out of a cabin in which he has been imprisoned, so that he can re-imprison himself in the cabin in the company of a huge grindstone. Who is to say which set of words is the better? Would a preference be based on anything other than a predilection already corrupted?

In pressing these questions, *Huckleberry Finn* anticipates the language games of *Ulysses* (1922) and much of Modernism. Its narrative voice functions as does Tiresias in *The Waste Land* (1922). I am thinking of Eliot's note to line 218:

> Tiresias, although a mere spectator and not indeed a 'character', is yet the most important personage in the poem, uniting all the rest. Just as the one-eyed merchant, seller of currants, melts into the Phoenician sailor, and the latter is not wholly distinct from Ferdinand Prince of Naples, so all the women are one woman, and the two sexes meet in Tiresias. What Tiresias *sees*, in fact, is the substance of the poem.

Huck too unites all the rest: Colonel Grangerford melting into Colonel Sherburn; Pap melting into the king and into Boggs; Jim, consciously or unconsciously, playing a variety of roles available to the black slave of his time. Were it not for the unceasing vitality of his humour, Twain, like Eliot, would have only fragments of culture to shore against ruin. He knows no language is self-evidently true. If only some of it were, Jim would never have been a slave.

8

James: *The American Scene* (1907)

I

'What shall we call our "self"? Where does it begin? Where does it end?' These questions about identity, voiced by the American Madame Merle in Chapter 19 of James's *The Portrait of a Lady* (1881), permeate nineteenth-century American literature. They concern not only personal and national identity, but also the identity of the literary works themselves. 'What shall we call our "self"? Where does it begin? Where does it end?' are questions novels and poems discussed in this book are asking about their own nature.

In search of answers on all three fronts, James committed himself to the Old World, as a place to live in and write about. His *Notebooks* for November 1881 insist that the American writer '*must* deal, more or less, even if only by implication, with Europe.'[1] What lay behind this declaration had been revealed in James's *Hawthorne* (1879). In this tribute to his compatriot, James argues nonetheless that Hawthorne's work remained undernourished, because Hawthorne in America did not have the advantages provided for a novelist by 'the denser, richer, warmer European spectacle'.[2] In Europe, it is implied, are structures of life and literature so validated by the long process of history, as to seem part of the impersonal system of things. There, the self might find objective confirmation of its identity. A literary work, joining traditions of other literary works, might be confident of its formal nature. The Old World seemed to offer relief from the New World's inescapable burden, unforgettably imagined by Melville: 'the intense concentration of self in the middle of such heartless immensity' (*Moby-Dick*, 'The Castaway').

Yet it is in Europe that the world-weary Madame Merle poses her questions to Isabel Archer, a younger version of her American self just arrived in the Old World. In Europe, Madame Merle has not found answers. Nor will Isabel Archer. Nor has James, even though *The Portrait of a Lady* in many of its areas seems remarkably confident about itself. This confidence is apparent in its seeming to have all 'the solidity of specification' that James, in 'The Art of Fiction' (1884), was to declare to be 'the supreme virtue of a novel'. In addition, *The Portrait of a Lady* is delivered to us by a James who, as 'The Art of Fiction' also recommends, speaks 'with assurance, with the tone of the historian'. These were qualities of the nineteenth-century European novel James had come to Europe to adopt. They contrast markedly with the 'something cold and light and thin, something belonging to the imagination alone' that James found in all of Hawthorne's writings.

The Portrait of a Lady, however, cannot sustain itself in this European guise, any more than its major characters can find a fulfilling identity in Europe. As James looked back on this novel in his 1907 Preface, he cited Chapter 42 as 'obviously the best thing in the book'. This chapter presents Isabel Archer's solitary night-time reflection on her marriage and on her life. It is a confirmation of how much *The Portrait of a Lady*, along with Isabel its central character, is moving away from the objective and the public towards the subjective and the private. This movement introduces the territory of most of James's subsequent work, where 'solidity of specification' in the material sense gives way to explorations of the subjective consciousness. Ironically, such territory turns out to be very close to what had been diagnosed critically in Hawthorne as 'something belonging to the imagination alone'.

Imagination and reality did not come together for James even in Europe, where he had certainly expected them to be capable of a relationship. In the Old World, reality became as unknowable as it always was in the New. The consequence for James was that he remained as imprisoned as any of his compatriots in the imagination and unending subjectivity.

It was a fate predicted by 'The Art of Fiction' itself, despite the essay's vouching at one stage for the historian's tone and for 'solidity of specification'. The very title, 'The Art of Fiction', like the title, *The Portrait of a Lady*, concedes everything to the imagination. Moreover, when James at another stage in the essay faces the recommendation that the writer should write from experience, he is compelled to ask:

> What kind of experience is intended, and where does it begin and end? Experience is never limited, and it is never complete; it

is an immense sensibility, a kind of huge spider-web of the finest silken threads suspended in the chamber of consciousness, and catching every air-borne particle in its tissue. It is the very atmosphere of the mind.

The questions in the first sentence here take us back to where we started with Madame Merle. What is asked of the self must also be asked of experience, because, as I tried to show in my reading of Dickinson's poem 528, knowledge of one is always dependent on knowledge of the other. Unless we can know where experience begins and ends we cannot know where the self begins and ends. These problems are all the more irresolvable when experience, as in 'The Art of Fiction' and during *The Portrait of a Lady*, loses its objective 'solidity of specification' and becomes 'the very atmosphere of the mind'.

In novel after novel James was to discover that the assurances of identity he sought in Europe were gone. European traditions were now no more sustaining on their own ground than they were when imported into America in, say, *Huckleberry Finn*. In fact it was to the vitality of America that Europe, as represented by a purposeless Lord Warburton in *The Portrait of a Lady* and a bereft Madame de Vionnet in *The Ambassadors* (1903), felt itself needing to turn. So, in *The American Scene*, James himself turned back to the New World after an absence of nearly twenty-five years.

II

What was James to call the self in the New World emerging into the twentieth century? The immigrants arriving daily were visible evidence of the impossibility of holding on to a definitive sense of what it was to be an American. In James they produced a 'sense of isolation', leading to the following rueful comment: 'It was not for this that the observer on whose behalf I more particularly write had sought to take up again the sweet sense of the natal air' (Chapter 3, ii).[3]

Notice the distinction here between 'the observer' and 'I'. In *The American Scene* we never discover who 'I' is, where it begins and ends. All we know are the various guises adopted by the 'observer'. Among these guises are the affectations of James's prose, as exemplified in a phrase such as 'the sweet sense of the natal air'.

For 'the observer' James creates at least twenty titles in addition to his favourite one, 'the restless analyst' (Chapter 1, i). These titles range from 'the cold-blooded critic' (Chapter 1, i), through 'the incurable eccentric' (Chapter 2, i), 'the perverted person' (Chapter 2, ii) and 'the starved story-seeker' (Chapter 7, iii), to 'the palpitating pilgrim' (Chapter 12, i). All of the titles serve, in Hawthorne's words from 'The Custom-House', to keep 'the inmost Me behind its veil'. The intention of both Hawthorne and James is to shield the 'inmost Me'. More significantly, it is also to conceal the fact that in an unknowable world the 'inmost Me' can never be found, not even by the writer himself.

It could not be found by Whitman either. Nonetheless, Whitman attempted to produce selves which were naturally responsive to, and harmonious with, the ever-changing New World. James, by contrast, advertises the estrangement of the titles he adopts. This estrangement is exaggerated and self-mocking, but at the same time it affects allegiance to an implied superior order of things belonging to the Old World. In this respect, James has not changed since *Hawthorne*. Chapter 1 of the earlier book tells us that, 'it takes a great deal of history to produce a little literature, that it needs a complex social machinery to set a writer in motion.' Now, in *The American Scene*, we read again that, 'It takes an endless amount of history to make even a little tradition, and an endless amount of tradition to make even a little taste, and an endless amount of taste, by the same token, to make even a little tranquillity' (Chapter 4, ii).

The rareness and scarcity of the final product in these pronouncements ('a little literature', 'a little tradition', 'a little taste', 'a little tranquillity') are also its exclusiveness. The final product is for the few, not for the many. Access to it and enjoyment of it enable the few to distinguish themselves from the many and to know who they are in relationship to the many. In contrast to this hierarchy, the New World embodies 'a democracy that, unlike the English, is social as well as political' (Chapter 7, iv), an important distinction still evident in the late twentieth century. As James is aware, this more thorough-going American democracy challenges Old World ideas of order. This challenge is exemplified at General Grant's tomb:

The tabernacle of Grant's ashes stands there by the pleasure-drive, unguarded and unenclosed, the feature of the prospect and the property of the people, as open as an hotel or a railway-station to any coming and going, and as dedicated to public use as builded things in America (when not mere closed churches) only can be. Unmistakable in its air of having had, all consciously, from the first, to raise its head and play its part without pomp and circumstance to 'back' it, without mystery or ceremony to protect it, without Church or State to intervene on its behalf, with only its immediacy, its familiarity of interest to circle it about, and only its proud outlook to preserve, so far as possible, its character. The tomb of Napoleon at the Invalides is a great national property, and the play of democratic manners sufficiently surrounds it; but as compared with the small pavilion on the Riverside bluff it is a holy of holies, a great temple jealously guarded and formally approached. And yet one doesn't conclude, strange to say, that the Riverside pavilion fails of its expression a whit more than the Paris dome; one perhaps even feels it triumph by its use of its want of reserve as a very last word. The admonition of all of which possibly is – I confess I but grope for it – that when there has been in such cases a certain other happy combination, an original sincerity of intention, an original propriety of site, and above all an original high value of name and fame, something in this line really supreme, publicity, familiarity, immediacy, as I have called them, *carried far enough*, may stalk in and out of the shrine with their hands in their pockets and their hats on their heads, and yet not dispel the Presence.

(Chapter 3, iv)

As is the case with most of the American literature discussed in this book, the creation of the monument to Grant is unaided by 'pomp and circumstance', 'mystery or ceremony', 'Church or State'. It was the trappings implied by such terms as these that James wanted to exploit for his own art in Europe. Art in America, when it has not imported European paraphernalia, has often had to depend, as in the case of Grant's tomb, on its 'immediacy' and 'original sincerity of intention'. The tomb, however, does have the advantage over the literature in its 'familiarity of interest' (to do with the recent Civil War) and 'the original high value of name and fame', belonging to Grant himself. The creator of the monument to Grant has not faced Melville's problem when creating Ahab: 'Oh, Ahab! what shall be grand in thee, it must needs be plucked at from the skies, and dived for in the deep, and featured in the unbodied air!' (*Moby-Dick*, 'The Specksynder').

Nonetheless, the monument is not allowed to exist in an exclusive formal world. So much is confirmed by the opening sentence of the above passage and by the comparison with the tomb of Napoleon. The monument is subjected to a 'play of democratic manners' more unrestrained in the New World than ever they are in the Old. As if modelling themselves on one of Whitman's poses, these manners have 'their hands in their pockets and their hats on their heads'. James, admittedly, has none of Whitman's exuberance on their behalf, and, on another occasion in *The American Scene*, 'the play of democratic manners' becomes, more fearfully, 'the monstrous form of Democracy' (Chapter 1, vi). Even so, James is fascinated by the radical challenge American democracy offers to the ways in which meaning has been historically constructed. His recognition of the success of Grant's tomb concludes with a question about America which is fundamental to the unsettled formal nature of the literature discussed in this book:

> Do certain impressions there represent the absolute extinction of old sensibilities, or do they represent only new forms of them? The inquiry would be doubtless easier to answer if so many of these feelings were not mainly known to us just by their attendant forms.

The energy and excitement of James's response to the New World in *The American Scene*, especially to the city of New York, have everything to do with the continuing irresolvability of his question. The 'appeal' of the city, as he gazes at its harbour, is 'of a particular kind of dauntless power':

> . . . it is the power of the most extravagant of cities, rejoicing, as with the voice of the morning, in its might, its fortune, its unsurpassable conditions, and imparting to every object and element, to the motion and expression of every floating, hurrying, panting thing, to the throb of ferries and tugs, to the plash of waves and play of winds and the glint of lights and the shrill of whistles and the quality and authority of breeze-born cries – all, practically, a diffused, wasted clamour of *detonations* – something of its sharp free accent and, above all, of its sovereign sense of being 'backed' and able to back. The universal *applied*

passion struck me as shining unprecedentedly out of the composition; in the bigness and bravery and insolence, especially, of everything that rushed and shrieked; in the air as of a great intricate frenzied dance, half merry, half desperate, or at least half defiant, performed on the huge water floor.

(Chapter 2, i).

As James lists the ingredients of this scene in the long opening sentence, one is reminded of Whitman's barely containable celebrations of the city. There is more energy here than ever James found in Europe. In response, James is himself so energised, that momentarily one feels that if ever he, or his characters, were to have escaped the confines of consciousness, it might have been by an extended confrontation of this New World. Not that such a feeling can be more than momentary. In American literature, there was a withdrawal into consciousness, or a protecting of the self by physically moving on, *because* the experience of the New World ('a great intricate frenzied dance') was so overwhelming. Despite numerous confident proclamations, no one could understand what the New World might mean. No one could conceive of its limits. 'What', as James puts it, 'would it ever say "no" to?' (Chapter 1, v). The road of the New World's possibilities was open and unending. Travelling along it, one might convince oneself with Whitman that one was participating in a democracy having divine inspiration. For his part, James can only believe that 'the main American formula' is 'to make so much money that you won't, that you don't "mind," don't mind anything' (Chapter 7, ii).

This creation of wealth can relieve poverty at one end of the scale and, at the other, build the Waldorf-Astoria. James acknowledges that 'there were grosser elements of the sordid and the squalid that I doubtless never saw' (Chapter 3, iii). Dickens had reported such elements in New York City sixty years earlier, but James is impressed in the city, as he is in the Country Clubs, by the material well-being of people who in their native lands would certainly be much worse off.[4] As for the Waldorf-Astoria, here James's 'charmed attention [moving] from one great chamber of the temple to another', transports us to an America Scott Fitzgerald is also to watch and wonder at twenty years later:

The question of who they all might be, seated under palms and by fountains, or communing, to some inimitable New York tune,

with the shade of Marie Antoinette in the queer recaptured
actuality of an easy Versailles or an intimate Trianon – such
questions as that, interesting in other societies and at other
times, insisted on yielding here to the mere eloquence of the
general truth. Here was a social order in positively stable equilibrium. Here was a world whose relation to its form and medium
was practically imperturbable; here was a conception of publicity
as the vital medium organized with the authority with which the
American genius for organization, put on its mettle, alone could
organize it. The whole thing remains for me, however, I repeat,
a gorgeous golden blur, a paradise peopled with unmistakable
American shapes.

(Chapter 2, iii)

As in the New York City of *The Great Gatsby* (1925) and the
Hollywood of *The Last Tycoon* (1941), America here has the wealth
and capacity for self-transformation to become anything: 'temple',
'Versailles', 'Trianon', 'paradise'. What it becomes may not be the
real thing, but who will know? Who will care? Who will remember
that there is a real thing, and, in any case, would it be any more
real than what the New World provides? If American life is the
perpetual masquerade also proclaimed in *The Blithedale Romance*
(1852), *The Confidence-Man* (1857) and *Huckleberry Finn*, why should
the bluff ever be called? Nineteenth-century American literature
reveals we are rarely dealing in the New World with illusion or
reality (the old European polarities), but with illusion or illusion.
There is no moment of truth, no arrival, no end except death.

On the personal scale the result is the absence of self-belief we
find in nineteenth-century American literature's many fugitive
voices. On the public scale, this absence is matched by James's
claim that 'The very sign of [New York's] energy is that it doesn't
believe in itself; it fails to succeed, even at a cost of millions, in
persuading you that it does' (Chapter 2, iii). The bluff may not be
called, but that it might not finally convince is suggested when
James reflects more forebodingly on the cast of characters, living in
what he now terms 'the universal Waldorf-Astoria':

Beguiled and caged, positively thankful, in its vast vacancy, for
the sense and the definite horizon of a cage, were there not yet
moments, were there not yet cases and connections, in which it

still dimly made out that its condition was the result of a compromise into the detail of which there might some day be an
alarm in entering?

(Chapter 14, iii)

Here we are at the opposite extreme from Thoreau's organic and
utilitarian model for the New World in *Walden* (1850). We have
another version of the people who are 'crazy and wild' for beguilement at the camp-meeting in Chapter 19 of *Huckleberry Finn*. The
'equilibrium' celebrated in the earlier passage is no longer 'positively stable'; nor is 'publicity' a 'vital medium'. What the 'alarm'
might be James does not reveal. Perhaps it is revealed in *An
American Tragedy* (1925), *The Great Gatsby* and *The Death of a Sales-
man* (1949).

The American Scene presents 'the great adventure of a society
reaching out into the apparent void' (Chapter 1, i), but James can
no more say what this adventure means than can the previous
writers in this book. New York City alone, he concludes, would
overwhelm the all-encompassing grasp even of a Zola. Into what
scheme of things could one fit an encounter on the very steps of
the Capitol in Washington between Henry James and 'a trio of
Indian braves'?

. . . braves dispossessed of forest and prairie, but as free of the
builded labyrinth as they had ever been of these; also arrayed in
neat pot-hats, shoddy suits and light overcoats, with their pockets,
I am sure, full of photographs and cigarettes: . . . They seemed just
then and there, for a mind fed betimes on the Leatherstocking
Tales, to project as in a flash an image in itself immense – reducing
to a single smooth stride the bloody footsteps of time. One rubbed
one's eyes, but there, at its highest polish, shining in the
beautiful day, was the brazen face of history, and there, all about
one, immaculate, the printless pavements of the state.

(Chapter 11,v)

What sense can be made of a history into which such fantastic
disjunctions as these are condensed? It may be that nothing more
can be done than to insist that the disjunctions are in fact *conjunc*-
tions. This insistence would amount to a declaration that what has
happened and what is happening are always their own justification.

'The bloody footsteps of time' are buried beneath the 'immaculate, the printless pavements of the state'. There is always, in other words, a new day, a new beginning. Such a declaration becomes in Whitman a celebratory fatalism and, faced with the unprecedented event of the New World, the footsteps of which could only have been bloody, one can appreciate the need for Whitman's posture. What is happening better be celebrated as good, because it cannot be arrested. There is no point of stasis from which to arrest.

The dispossession of the Indian braves is succeeded by James's own 'sense of dispossession' when he visits Ellis Island and sees the 'drama [of the arriving immigrants] that goes on, without pause, day by day and year by year'. Returning to Washington Square, he finds the family home gone and feels 'amputated of half my history' (Chapter 2, ii). These are not the words of a man who could ever assume Whitman's celebratory stance in the face of the New World's insistent present tense. Like Hawthorne, James clings to the past to stake out an identity. Our suspicions of Hawthorne's claim on his forbears in 'The Custom-House' preface to *The Scarlet Letter*, however, are greatly increased in the case of James's protestations about a history of which he has been the absentee landlord for nearly a quarter of a century. In the American scene identity is always posture, because no one knows the meaning of where they are. Assuming a representative third person stance (wanting to speak for us all as much as Whitman also does), James finally confesses:

> He doesn't *know*, he can't say, before the facts, and he doesn't even want to know or to say; the facts themselves loom, before the understanding, in too large a mass for a mere mouthful: it is as if the syllables were too numerous to make a legible word. The *il*legible word, accordingly, the great inscrutable answer to questions, hangs in the vast American sky, to his imagination, as something fantastic and *abracadabrant*, belonging to no known language.
>
> (Chapter 3, i)

This pronouncement commands such authority as a response to the American scene, that it might serve as an authorial preface to all the works of American literature discussed in this book. We have the reasons here for the literature's fundamental and immediate problems with language and structure. We have also James's

unsurpassable term for the languages and structures American
writers produced: 'something fantastic and *abracadabrant*'.

III

It might have been expected that there would be a 'legible word' in
the American South. 'How', James asks, 'was the sight of Richmond not to be a potent idea'? It had been invested by the war
'with one of the great reverberating historic names'. It and other
Southern cities hung 'together on the dreadful page, the cities of
the supreme holocaust, the final massacres, the blood, the flames,
the tears' (Chapter 12, ii).

Yet the cities of Richmond and Charleston look to James 'simply
blank and void' (Chapter 12, ii). In the North this condition had to
do with the unprecedented and the undemarcated. In the South it
is the legacy of a past that has been a monumental aberration:

> . . . the very essence of the old Southern idea – the hugest
> fallacy, as it hovered there to one's backward, one's ranging
> vision, for which hundreds of thousands of men had ever laid
> down their lives. I was tasting of the very bitterness of the
> immense, grotesque, defeated project – the project, extravagant,
> fantastic, and today pathetic in its folly, of a vast Slave State (as
> the old term ran) artfully, savingly isolated in the world that was
> to contain it and trade with it. This was what everything around
> me meant – that the absurdity had once flourished there.
>
> (Chapter 12, ii)

From this basis James's understanding of the South reaches forward twenty years towards Faulkner. In Richmond's Museum of
the Confederacy, he is filled with wonder at the thought of having
'this great melancholy void to garnish and to people' (Chapter 12,
iii). Such a phrase goes a long way in explaining the 'something
fantastic and *abracadabrant*' in the later Southern writer. One of
James's personifications of the South might indeed be Rosa Cold-
field from *Absalom, Absalom!* (1936):

> . . . a figure somehow blighted or stricken, discomfortably,
> impossibly seated in an invalid-chair, and yet fixing one with
> strange eyes that were half a defiance and half a deprecation of

one's noticing, and much more of one's referring to, any abnormal sign . . . my haunting similitude was an image of the keeping-up of appearances, and above all of the maintainance of tone, the historic 'high' tone, in an excruciating posture. There was food for sympathy.

(Chapter 12, ii)

The sympathy is for a South 'condemned . . . to . . . a horrid heritage she had never consciously invited' (Chapter 12, ii). This heritage derives from a history which, in the first quotation of this section, is a revelation of 'fallacy', 'folly' and 'absurdity'. Applied to the attempt to found 'a vast Slave State', this sense of the past is arguably too indulgent towards people who might be regarded as perpetrators rather than victims. It lacks the unremitting condemnation many would feel to be obligatory. Great writers moralise, however, only to be inclusive, recognising as all too human whatever humanity has done. The past has always been lived by people like ourselves.

'I look down towards his feet, but that's a fable.' With these words at the end of the play, Othello acknowledges that Iago is not a monster or a devil. Similarly, in Chapter 27 of *The Confidence-Man* Melville tells us: 'Nearly all Indian-haters have at bottom loving hearts.' For his part, James reports meeting in the museum at Richmond 'a son of the new South . . . intelligent and humorous and highly conversable . . . He was a fine contemporary young American, incapable, so to speak, of hurting a Nothern fly – *as* Northern.' Nonetheless, 'there were things (ah, we had touched on some of these!) that all fair, engaging, smiling, as he stood there, he would have done to a Southern negro' (Chapter 12, iii).

Unconsoled by history, American literary figures before and since James have turned to Nature for solace. In James's words,

One was liable, in the States, on many a scene, to react, as it were, from the people, and to throw oneself passionately on the bosom of contiguous Nature, whatever surface it might happen to offer; one was apt to be moved, in possibly almost invidious preference, or in deeper and sweeter confidence, to try what may be made of *that*.

(Chapter 14, ii)

Not that nature will be more than a passing temptation. Typically for James, the very manner of this prose is so far removed from any naturalness of expression, that in itself it confesses the futility of the venture it proposes. Even as he suggests a possibility, James wants to foreclose it, and in this tactic there is, despite the self-mockery, an element of defensiveness. In Florida, it is true, he can write of 'all the succulence of the admirable pale-skinned orange and the huge sun-warmed grape-fruit, plucked from the low bough, where it fairly bumps your cheek for solicitation'. Nonetheless, the conclusion to this foretaste of the sensuous betrays alarm and even fear:

> . . . *this*, I said, was sub-tropical Florida – and doubtless as permitted a glimpse as I should ever have of any such effect. The softness was divine – like something mixed, in a huge silver crucible, as an elixir, and then liquidly scattered. But the refine-ment of the experience would be the summer noon or the summer night – it would be then the breast of Nature would open; save only that so lost in it and with such lubrication of surrender, how should one ever come back?
>
> (Chapter 14, v)

Not for James the risk of the eventual fate of one of his literary descendents, Pound's Mauberley:

> I was
> And I no more exist;
> Here drifted
> An hedonist.

IV

In the closing paragraphs of *The American Scene* we return again to the New World's insufficiency of 'History', which means also the insufficiency of a shaping cultural heritage. James continues:

> . . . how grimly, meanwhile, under the annual rigour, the world, for the most part, waits to be less ugly again, less despoiled of interest, less abandoned to monotony, less forsaken of the presence that forms its only resource, of the one friend to

whom it owes all it ever gets, of the pitying season that shall save it from its huge insignificance.

These words accompany James's journey northwards by Pullman at the end of winter, spring being 'the pitying season'. They remind us how close to the edge of desolation James performed as an artist, and how consciously and deliberately his art *made* the life he needed. When he goes on to write, 'If I were one of the painted savages', and 'if I had been a beautiful red man with a tomahawk', his imagining of these further identities for the self is always a recognition of their impossibility. Of all the writers in this book James, along with Poe, was at the furthest remove from any naturalness of intercourse and harmony with what he now terms 'the great lonely land'.

This last expression is used in reaction against the 'hideous and unashamed' spread of American civilisation, as evidenced by the all-conquering Pullman in which James travels. In the last lines of *The American Scene*, he longs for 'an unbridgeable abyss or an insuperable mountain'. By this stage his only remaining title is that of 'the lone observer', the common identity which is no identity of nineteenth-century American literary voices. It confirms the fugitive; but the Pullman is not the raft and 'territory ahead' cannot now be spoken of.

Notes

1 COOPER: *THE LEATHER-STOCKING TALES*

1. All quotations from *The Pioneers* are from the Penguin edition (Harmondsworth, 1988). Chapter numbers in brackets refer to this edition.
2. The quotation is from *Notions of the Americans Picked Up By A Travelling Bachelor* (1828). The relevant pages dealing with 'The Literature and Arts of the United States' are widely anthologised. See, for example, *The Norton Anthology of American Literature*, Vol. I, second edition (New York, London, 1985), pp. 763–77.
3. *Love and Death in the American Novel* (New York, 1960; London, 1961) Chapter 6. All further quotations are from this chapter.
4. The phrase is from Part 14 of 'When Lilacs Last in the Dooryard Bloom'd'.
5. *Richard II*, I.iii. 275–80, The Arden Shakespeare (London, 1956).
6. *Studies in Classic American Literature* (London, 1924), Chapter 5. All further quotations are from this chapter.
7. Donald Davie, *The Heyday of Sir Walter Scott* (London: 1961), p. 143.
8. See Emerson's *Nature* (1836), Chapter 4.
9. Henry Nash Smith, *Virgin Land: The American West as Symbol and Myth* (Cambridge, Mass., 1950), Chapter 6.
10. *The Tempest*, I.ii. 333–4, The Arden Shakespeare (London, 1954).
11. See Davie, op. cit., and George Dekker, *James Fenimore Cooper The Novelist* (London, 1967).
12. Scott's essay can be found in *The Miscellaneous Prose Works of Sir Walter Scott*, Vol. VI (Edinburgh and London, 1834), pp. 129–216.
13. All quotations from *The Last of the Mohicans* are from the Penguin edition (Harmondsworth, 1986). Chapter numbers in brackets refer to this edition.
14. Henry Nash Smith makes this point in his Introduction to the Rinehart edition of *The Prairie* (New York, 1950).
15. *The Merchant of Venice*, III.i. 52–66, The Arden Shakespeare (London, 1959).
16. Dekker, op. cit. pp. 69–72.
17. Davie, op. cit., pp. 105–11.
18. *Heart of Darkness* (1902), Chapter 2.
19. All quotations from *The Prairie* are from the Penguin edition (Harmondsworth, 1988). Chapter numbers in brackets refer to this edition.
20. Introduction to the Rinehart edition of *The Prairie*.
21. All quotations from *The Deerslayer* are from the Penguin edition (Harmondsworth, 1988). Chapter numbers refer to this edition.
22. See 'Fenimore Cooper and the Ruins of Time', in *In Defense of Reason* (New York, 1947).

2 POE'S FICTION: *ARTHUR GORDON PYM* TO 'THE BLACK CAT'

1. All quotations from *Arthur Gordon Pym* are taken from the Penguin edition (1975). The chapter numbers after quotations refer to this edition.
2. Henry James, *The Portrait of a Lady* (1881), Chapter 19.
3. *The Power of Blackness* (New York, 1958), Chapter 4.
4. *Hawthorne* (London, 1879), Chapter 2.
5. *Studies in Classic American Literature* (London, 1924), Chapter 6.
6. All quotations from the poems and stories are taken from *The Fall of the House of Usher and Other Writings* (Penguin: 1986).
7. This quotation has never been found in Glanvill.
8. 'Reflections on and in "The Fall of the House of Usher"' in A. R. Lee (ed.), *Edgar Allan Poe: The Design of Order* (London and New Jersey, 1987), p. 27.
9. *Moby Dick* (1851), Chapter 35.
10. 'Was the Chevalier Left-Handed? Poe's Dupin Stories', in Lee, op. cit., p. 92.
11. *Macbeth*, V.v. 26–8, The Arden Shakespeare (London and New York, 1959). All further references to *Macbeth* will be to this edition.
12. *The Power of Blackness*, Chapter 5.
13. *Notes From Underground*, translated by Jessie Coulson (Penguin, 1972), p. 26.
14. All quotations from *Eureka* are from *The Science Fiction of Edgar Allan Poe* (Penguin, 1976). Page numbers refer to this edition.

3 HAWTHORNE: *THE SCARLET LETTER* (1850)

1. For a recent account of Scott's contribution to historical narrative both as historian and as novelist see George Dekker, *The American Historical Romance* (Cambridge, New York, Melbourne, 1987), pp. 29ff. In Chapter 7 of his book Dekker makes detailed comparisons between *The Heart of Midlothian* and *The Scarlet Letter*. His purpose and his conclusions, however, are different from mine.
2. All quotations are from the Penguin edition of *The Scarlet Letter* (1970). Numbers in brackets refer to chapters in this edition.
3. 'Hawthorne and His Mosses' (1850). This well known essay is reprinted in most anthologies of nineteenth-century American literature.
4. *Hawthorne* (London, 1879), Chapter 3.
5. See the essay, 'Maule's Curse, or Hawthorne and the Problem of Allegory', in *In Defense of Reason* (New York, 1947).
6. See Scott's 'An Essay on Romance' (1824). It may be found in *The Miscellaneous Prose Works of Sir Walter Scott*, Vol. 6 (Edinburgh and London, 1834), pp. 129–216.
7. See Cooper's *Notions of the Americans* (1828), especially the widely anthologised section dealing with the literature and arts of the United States.

8. D. H. Lawrence *Studies in Classic American Literature* (London, 1924), Chapter 7.
9. Charles Feidelson, Jr, *Symbolism and American Literature* (Phoenix edition, Chicago, 1959), p. 10.
10. I. Williams (ed.), *Sir Walter Scott on Novelists and Fiction* (London, 1968), p. 116.
11. *The American Historical Romance*, op. cit., p. 253.
12. Sandra M. Gilbert and Susan Gubar, *The Madwoman in the Attic: The Woman Writer in the Nineteenth Century Literary Imagination* (New Haven and London, 1979), p. 12.
13. *Hawthorne*, Chapter 5.

4 MELVILLE: *MOBY-DICK* (1851)

1. All quotations are from the Penguin edition of *Moby-Dick* (1970). Chapter numbers in brackets refer to chapters in this edition.
2. According to James the American writer's consolation, amid all the deprivations, was 'that "American humour" of which of later years we have heard so much'. *Hawthorne* (London, 1879), Chapter 2.
3. Compare 'All visible things are emblems', *Sartor Resartus*, Book I, Chapter 11. Melville was obviously tangling with the Transcendentalism of both Carlyle and Emerson.
4. *King Lear*, III.iv. 109, The Arden Edition (London and Massachusetts, 1957).
5. *Hamlet*, I.iv. 81, The Arden Edition (London and New York, 1982).
6. The review, 'Hawthorne and his Mosses' (1850) is widely reprinted in anthologies of American literature.
7. See Emerson's *Nature* (1836), the last paragraph of the Introduction. It is widely reprinted in anthologies of American literature.
8. *Walden* (1850), Chapter 2.
9. *American Renaissance: Art and Expression in the Age of Emerson and Whitman* (London, New York, Toronto, 1941), p. 426.
10. *Studies in Classic American Literature* (London, 1924), Chapter 11.
11. Leslie Fiedler deals at length with Ishmael/Queequeg, Ahab/Fedallah in his chapter on *Moby-Dick* in *Love and Death in the American Novel* (New York, 1960).
12. The lines are from 'I felt a Funeral, in my Brain', poem 280 in Thomas H. Johson (ed.), *Emily Dickinson: The Complete Poems* (London, 1970).

5 WHITMAN: *LEAVES OF GRASS*

1. For the most part, I shall be dealing with Whitman's poems in the chronological order of their publication in the various editions of *Leaves of Grass*, but in their final text form.
2. *The Prelude*, Book XIII, line 276.
3. James uses the phrase as he stands before the tomb of General Grant in Chapter 3 of *The American Scene* (London, 1907). At this moment he

finds himself asking of the New World the central question: 'Do certain impressions there represent the absolute extinction of old sensibilities, or do they represent only new forms of them? The inquiry would be doubtless easier to answer if so many of these feelings were not mainly known to us just *by* their attendant forms.'

4. The numbers in brackets refer to the poems of 'Song of Myself'.
5. See Eliot's essay, '*Ulysses*, Order and Myth', *The Dial* (November, 1923).
6. For an authoritative celebration of Whitman as a language maker see Randall Jarrell's 'Some Lines from Whitman'. This essay is reprinted in Boris Ford (ed.), *The New Pelican Guide to English Literature: 9, American Literature* (London, 1988), pp. 139–52.
7. 'Clusters' was the name Whitman gave to the various groupings of poems in *Leaves of Grass*, beginning with the 1860 edition.
8. As well as the Preface, the 1855 *Leaves of Grass* comprised: 'Song of Myself', 'A Song for Occupations', 'To Think of Time', 'The Sleepers', 'I Sing the Body Electric', 'Faces', 'Song of the Answerer', 'Europe, The 72d and 73d Years of These States', 'A Boston Ballad', 'There Was a Child Went Forth', 'Who Learns My Lesson Complete', 'Great Are the Myths'.
9. Charles Feidelson, Jr, *Symbolism and American Literature* (Chicago and London: 1953), p. 27. In other respects, Feidelson's is a very perceptive treatment of Whitman.
10. Richard Chase, *Walt Whitman Reconsidered* (New York, 1955), p. 34.
11. M. Wynn Thomas, *The Lunar Light of Whitman's Poetry* (Cambridge, Mass., and London, 1987), p. 198.
12. F. O. Matthiessen, *The American Renaissance: Art and Expression in the Age of Emerson and Whitman* (London, New York, Toronto, 1941), p. 517.
13. *The American Scene*, the last paragraph of Chapter 2.
14. *Studies in Classic American Literature* (London, 1924).
15. *The House of the Seven Gables* (1851), Chapter 10.

6 DICKINSON'S POETRY

1. The numbers identifying the poems are Thomas H. Johnson's numbering in his *The Poems of Emily Dickinson* (Cambridge, Mass., 1963). All quotations are from this edition.
2. For an important essay on this poem see Albert Gelpi, 'Emily Dickinson and the Deerslayer: The Dilemma of the Woman Poet in America'. The essay appears in Sandra M. Gilbert and Susan Gubar (eds) *Shakespeare's Sisters: Feminist Essays on Women Poets* (Bloomington and London, 1979).
3. Arthur Sherbo (ed.), *Johnson on Shakespeare* (New Haven and London, 1968), p. 431.
4. *Moby-Dick*, 'The Castaway'.
5. Vesuvius at Home: The Power of Emily Dickinson' in Gilbert and Gubar, op. cit., p. 107.
6. See Poe's 1839 'Preface' to *Tales of the Grotesque and Arabesque*. It can be

found in I. M. Walker (ed.), *Edgar Allan Poe: The Critical Heritage* (London and New York, 1986), pp. 115–16.

7. *Emily Dickinson: The Mind of the Poet* (Norton Library Edition, New York, 1971), p. 113.

8. Sandra M. Gilbert and Susan Gubar, *The Madwoman in the Attic: The Woman Writer in the Nineteenth Century Literary Imagination* (New Haven and London, 1979), p. 646.

9. Wallace Stevens, *Notes Toward a Supreme Fiction*, 'It Must Be Abstract', poem 4.

10. Nathaniel Hawthorne, *The House of the Seven Gables* (1851), Chapter 10.

7 TWAIN: *ADVENTURES OF HUCKLEBERRY FINN* (1884)

1. All quotations are taken from the Penguin edition of *Adventures of Huckleberry Finn* (1966). Chapter numbers refer to this edition.

2. See Smith's Introduction to the Riverside Press edition of *Adventures of Huckleberry Finn* (Cambridge, Mass., 1958) and Blair's *Mark Twain and Huck Finn* (Berkeley and Los Angeles, 1962). All further references to Smith and Blair will be to these books. For two recent readings of Huck as a character see James L. Kastely, 'The Ethics of Self Interest: Narrative Logic', in *Huckleberry Finn, Nineteenth Century Fiction*, Vol. 40 (June, 1985), pp. 412–37; also Tim William Machen, 'The Symbolic Narrative of *Huckleberry Finn*', *Arizona Quarterly*, Vol. 42 (Summer, 1986), pp. 130–40.

3. Leslie A. Fiedler, *Love and Death in the American Novel* (New York, 1960). The further reference to Fiedler is also to his chapter on *Huckleberry Finn* in this book.

4. Richard Poirier, *A World Elsewhere: The Place of Style in American Literature* (London, Oxford, New York, 1966), Chapter 4. The further reference to Poirier is also to this chapter.

5. The authoritative account of when Twain wrote *Huckleberry Finn* is in Blair, op. cit.

8 JAMES: *THE AMERICAN SCENE* (1907)

1. F. O. Matthiessen and Kenneth B. Murdock (eds), *The Notebooks of Henry James* (New York, 1947), p. 24.

2. *Hawthorne* (1879), Chapter 2. All further quotations from this book are from this chapter.

3. All quotations from *The American Scene* are from the first English edition (London, 1907).

4. I find that Edel misrepresents James's response to poverty in New York. When James writes of the 'freedom to grow up to be blighted' (Chapter 3, iii), it is not, as Edel implies, poverty he is referring to, but the powerlessness of people in the hands of 'Trusts' and 'new remorseless monopolies'. Leon Edel, *The Life of Henry James* (Penguin, 1977), p. 600.

Select Bibliography

To begin to establish a comprehensive sense of American literature readers should consult a standard anthology such as *The Norton Anthology of American Literature* (3rd edn, 1989). Volume 1 begins with seventeenth century literature and ends with Emily Dickinson. Volume 2 begins with Mark Twain and comes through to the late twentieth century.

Accounts of scholarship and criticism, up to 1969, concerning Poe, Hawthorne, Melville, Whitman, Twain and James can be found in James Woodress (ed.), *Eight American Authors: a Review of Research and Criticism* (1971). Similar information on Cooper and Dickinson is in Robert A. Rees and Earl N. Harbert (eds), *Fifteen American Authors Before 1900: Bibliographic Essays on Research and Criticism*. The periodical, *American Literature: A Journal of Literary History, Criticism, and Bibliography*, maintains a selected bibliography of articles on American literature, as they appear.

JAMES FENIMORE COOPER (1789–1851)

The Writings of James Fenimore Cooper (1985–), with James Franklin Beard as editor-in-chief, will become the standard edition of Cooper's work. Beard has edited *Letters and Journals of James Fenimore Cooper* (6 volumes, 1960–68). A biography is forthcoming. Among other biographies are James Grossman, *James Fenimore Cooper* (1949) and Robert E. Spiller, *Fenimore Cooper: Critic of His Time* (1931).
Further critical reading would include:

Donald Davie	*The Heyday of Sir Walter Scott* (1961)
George Dekker and	
John P. Macwilliams (eds)	*Fenimore Cooper: The Critical Heritage* (1973)
George Dekker	*James Fenimore Cooper The Novelist* (1964)
H. Daniel Peck	*A World By Itself: The Pastoral Moment in Cooper's Fiction* (1977)

EDGAR ALLAN POE (1809–49)

Thomas O. Mabbot's projected edition of *Collected Works of Edgar Allan Poe* (1978–) is likely to become the standard edition. *The Letters of Edgar Allan Poe* have been edited by W. Ostrom in 1948 and again (with additional letters) in 1966. Accounts of Poe's life have had to penetrate a notorious maze of fact and fiction. An invaluable guide is provided by Dwight Thomas and David K. Jackson (eds), *The Poe Log: A Documentary Life of Edgar Allan Poe* (1987). Further critical reading would include:

Jean Alexander	*Affidavits of Genius: Edgar Allan Poe and the French Critics, 1847–1924* (1971)

Joan Dayan	*Fables of the Mind: an Inquiry into Poe's Fiction* (1987)
William L. Howarth	*Twentieth Century Interpretations of Poe's Tales* (1971)
A. R. Lee (ed.)	*Edgar Allan Poe: The Design of Order* (1987)
Robert Regan (ed.)	*Poe: A Collection of Critical Essays* (1967)

NATHANIEL HAWTHORNE (1804–64)

The Centenary Edition of Hawthorne (1963–) is the standard edition. L. Neal Smith and Thomas Woodson have edited the *Letters* (4 volumes, 1984–7). The standard biography is Randall Stewart, *Nathaniel Hawthorne: A Biography* (1948). See also Rita Gollin, *Portraits of Nathaniel Hawthorne* (1983), and James Mellow, *Nathaniel Hawthorne in His Times* (1980). Examples of the critical work on Hawthorne are:

Nina Baym	*The Shape of Hawthorne's Career* (1976)
J. Donald Crowley (ed.)	*Hawthorne: The Critical Heritage* (1970)
	Nathaniel Hawthorne: A Collection of Criticism (1975)
Frederick C. Crews	*The Sins of the Fathers: Hawthorne's Psychological Themes* (1966)
George Dekker	*The American Historical Romance* (1987)
Henry James	*Hawthorne* (1879)
A. N. Kaul (ed.)	*Hawthorne: A Collection of Critical Essays* (1966)
R. H. Pearce (ed.)	*Hawthorne Centenary essays* (1964)

HERMAN MELVILLE (1819–91)

The standard edition is the Northwestern-Newberry edition of *The Writings of Herman Melville* (1968–), Harrison Hayford, Hershel Parker and G. Thomas Tansell (eds). It includes the *Letters*. The standard biography is Leon Howard, *Herman Melville: A Biography* (1951). Essential biographical documents are collected in Jay Leda, *The Melville Log* (1951, revised and supplemented, 1969, further revision and supplements impending). Critical reading would include:

Watson G. Branch (ed.)	*Melville: The Critical Heritage* (1974)
Edgar A. Dryden	*Melville's Thematics of Form: The Great Art of Telling the Truth* (1968)
Tyrus Hillway and Luther S. Mansfield	*'Moby-Dick': Centennial Essays* (1953)
Hershel Parker and Harrison Hayford	*'Moby-Dick' as Doubloon* (1970)
Merton M. Sealts	*Pursuing Melville: 1940–80* (1982)

WALT WHITMAN (1819–92)

The Collected Writings of Walt Whitman (1961–) with Gay Wilson Allen and
Sculley Bradley as editors-in-chief include *The Correspondence*. Sculley
Bradley, Harold W. Blodgett, Arthur Golden and William White (eds)
'Leaves of Grass': A Textual Variorum of the Printed Poems (3 volumes, 1980) is
essential. Allen's *The Solitary Singer* (rev. edn, 1967) is the standard
biography, but there is also Justin Kaplan's *Walt Whitman: A Life* (1980).
Critical reading includes:

Gay Wilson Allen	*New Walt Whitman Handbook* (1975)
Milton Hindus	*Whitman: The Critical Heritage* (1971)
R. W. B. Lewis (ed.)	*The Presence of Walt Whitman* (1962)
R. H. Pearce (ed.)	*Whitman: A Collection of Critical Essays* (1962)
M. Wynn Thomas	*The Lunar Light of Whitman's Poetry* (1987)
Paul Zweig	*Walt Whitman: The Making of the Poet* (1984)

EMILY DICKINSON (1830–86)

The standard text is Thomas H. Johnson, *The Poems of Emily Dickinson*
(3 volumes, 1955). Along with Theodora Ward, Johnson has also edited *The
Letters of Emily Dickinson* (3 volumes, 1958). R. W. Franklin, *The Manuscript
Books of Emily Dickinson* (2 volumes, 1981) provides facsimiles of the
handsewn fascicles of the poems as they were left by Dickinson. Johnson's
Emily Dickinson: an Interpretative Biography (1955) is the standard biogra-
phy, but see also Richard B. Sewall, *The Life of Emily Dickinson* (1974).
Examples of the criticism are:

Charles R. Anderson	*Emily Dickinson's Poetry* (1960)
Richard Chase	*Emily Dickinson* (1951)
Albert J. Gelpi	*Emily Dickinson: The Mind of the Poet* (1965)
Sandra M. Gilbert and Susan Gubar	*The Madwoman in the Attic: The Woman Writer and the Nineteenth Century Literary Imagination* (1979)
Susan Juhasz (ed.)	*Feminist Critics Read Emily Dickinson* (1983)

MARK TWAIN (1835–1910)

Albert Bigelow Paine (ed.), *The Writings of Mark Twain*, (37 volumes,
1922–25) is the standard edition. It is being replaced by Robert Hirst (ed.),
The Mark Twain Papers (1969–) and by John Gerber (ed.), *The Works of Mark
Twain* (1972–). The most reliable biographies are Justin Kaplan, *Mr
Clemens and Mark Twain* (1966) and Everett Emerson, *The Authentic Mark
Twain: A Literary Biography of Samuel L. Clemens* (1985). The biography of

Twain remains a vexed issue and is full of lively problems. His *Autobiography* has been differently edited by Paine (1924), Bernard De Voto (1940) and Charles Neider (1959). In addition, there is Paine's *Mark Twain, a Biography* (1912). Willian Dean Howell's *My Mark Twain* (1910) is a fascinating personal tribute. Critical reading should include:

Walter Blair	*Mark Twain and Huckleberry Finn* (1960)
Bernard De Voto	*Mark Twain's America* (1932)
	Mark Twain at Work (1942)
James Cox	*Mark Twain: The Fate of Humour* (1966)
Henry Nash Smith	*Mark Twain: The Development of a Writer* (1962)

HENRY JAMES (1843–1916)

The Novels and Tales of Henry James (26 volumes, 1907–17, re-issued 1962–65) is the celebrated New York Edition. It comprises James's re-writing of work already published but omits much of that work. Leon Edel has edited *The Complete Plays of Henry James* (1949), F. O. Matthiessen and Kenneth B. Murdoch *The Notebooks of Henry James* (1947), and F. W. Dupee *Henry James: Autobiography* (3 volumes, 1956). Edel has written a definitive but problematically Freudian biography, *The Life of Henry James* (5 volumes, 1953–72, re-issued by Penguin, 2 volumes, 1977). F. O. Matthiessen's *The James Family* (1947) is also important biographically. Examples from an immense amount of criticism are:

Quentin Anderson	*The American Henry James* (1957)
Nicola Bradbury	*Henry James: The Later Novels* (1979)
F. W. Dupee	*Henry James* (1951)
Dorothea Krook	*The Ordeal of Consciousness in Henry James* (1962)
F. O. Matthiessen	*Henry James: The Major Phase* (1944)
Richard Poirier	*The Comic Sense of Henry James* (1960)
Viola Hopkins Winner	*Henry James and the Visual Arts* (1970)

The following is a list of works which consider some or all of the texts discussed in this book. Those by Chase, Fiedler, Feidelson, Lawrence, Matthiessen, Pearce, Poirier, Smith, and Winters have become the foundation stones of the criticism of nineteenth-century American literature. Lawrence and Matthiessen, especially, are essential reading.

Richard Chase	*The American Novel and Its Tradition* (1957)
Charles Feidelson, Jr	*Symbolism and American Literature* (1953)
Leslie Fiedler	*Love and Death in the American Novel* (2nd edn, 1966)
Martin Green	*Re-Appraisals: Some Commonsense Readings in American Literature* (1963)
D. H. Lawrence	*Studies in Classic American Literature* (1924)

Harry Levin   *The Power of Blackness* (1958)
R. W. B. Lewis   *The American Adam* (1955)
Leo Marx   *The Machine in the Garden* (1967)
F. O. Matthiessen   *The American Renaissance: Art and Expression
                               in the Age of Emerson and Whitman* (1941)
Wright Morris   *The Territory Ahead* (1957)
Roy Harvey Pearce   *The Continuity of American Poetry* (1961)
Richard Poirier   *A World Elsewhere: The Place of Style in
                               American Literature* (1966)
David S. Reynolds   *Beneath the American Renaissance: The
                               Subversive Imagination in the Age of
                               Emerson and Melville* (1988)
Henry Nash Smith   *Virgin Land: The American West as Symbol
                               and Myth* (1950)
Tony Tanner   *The Reign of Wonder: Naivety and Reality in
                               American Literature* (1965)
William Carlos Williams   *In the American Grain* (1966)
Yvor Winters   *In Defense of Reason* (1947)

Index